AN INTRODUCTION TO THE
CHINESE ECONOMY

THE DRIVING FORCES BEHIND MODERN DAY CHINA

AN INTRODUCTION TO THE
CHINESE ECONOMY

THE DRIVING FORCES BEHIND MODERN DAY CHINA

Rongxing Guo

WILEY
John Wiley & Sons (Asia) Pte. Ltd.

Other Wiley Editorial Offices

John Wiley & Sons, 111 River Street, Hoboken, NJ 07030, USA

John Wiley & Sons, The Atrium, Southern Gate, Chichester, West Sussex, P019 8SQ, United Kingdom

John Wiley & Sons (Canada) Ltd., 5353 Dundas Street West, Suite 400, Toronto, Ontario, M9B 6HB, Canada

John Wiley & Sons Australia Ltd., 42 McDougall Street, Milton, Queensland 4064, Australia Wiley-VCH, Boschstrasse 12, D-69469 Weinheim, Germany

Library of Congress Cataloging-in-Publication Data

ISBN 978-0-470-82604-1

Typeset in 10.5/14pt MinionPro-Regular by Thomson Digital, India

Printed in Singapore by Saik Wah Press Pte. Ltd.

10 9 8 7 6 5 4 3 2 1

To Fan Zhongjie (1932–)
my mother-in-law, who cares for her grandchildren
(Yanni, Maomao, Changchang, and Yaqing)
with all her heart and love

CONTENTS

List of figures, tables, and abbreviations

List of Figures

List of Tables

List of Abbreviations

CCP	Chinese Communist Party
CCPCC	Chinese Communist Party Central Committee
COE	collectively owned enterprise
CPE	centrally planned economy
CPPCC	Chinese People's Political Consultative Congress
FDI	foreign direct investment
FIE	foreign-invested enterprise (including Taiwan, Hong Kong, and Macau) invested enterprise
GDP	gross domestic product
GHG	greenhouse gas
GNP	gross national product
HRS	household responsibility system
NBS	National Bureau of Statistics of China
NIE	newly industrialized economy
NPC	National People's Congress
PCS	people's commune system
PPP	purchasing power parity
PRC	People's Republic of China
PSE	private, shareholding or other enterprise
RMB	Renminbi (Chinese currency)
SAR	special administrative region
SARS	severe acute respiratory syndrome
SEZ	special economic zone
SOE	state-owned enterprise
WTO	World Trade Organization

ACKNOWLEDGMENTS

Frankly speaking, it is not an easy task to write an introductory text, including the spatial characteristics and growth process in economies as *sui generis* and complex as that of China. Fortunately, my continuous interest in the working mechanism—at both macro and micro levels—of the Chinese economy, on the one hand, and the encouragement received from Mr. Nick Wallwork (Publisher of John Wiley & Sons Asia Pte. Ltd.), on the other hand, have enabled this project to be completed without delay. Definitely, without Ms. Jules Yap (Editorial Executive) and Ms. Fiona Wong (Production Editor), my communication and cooperation with the publisher would not have been so smooth, efficient, and productive. Also, Ms. Wong helped me clarify copyright issues and provided sources of the photos that have been adopted in this book. Mr. Edward Caruso did an excellent job in copyediting this book.

During the production stage of this book, I received excellent service and help at the Brookings Institution (Washington, D.C.) where I was a Visiting Fellow at the Center for Northeast Asian Policy Studies (CNAPS). Obviously, this made the revision and the proofreading of this book a smooth process. Dr. Richard Bush (Senior Fellow and Director of CNAPS), Mr. Kevin Scott (CNAPS Senior Assistant Director), and Ms. Jennifer Mason (CNAPS Research Assistant), among the others, merit particular mention.

Last but not least, I must acknowledge the external reviewers, including Professor Pieter Bottelier (Johns Hopkins University SAIS) whose comments and suggestions have helped me to make the final revision (correction) of this book. However, all views, drawbacks, and errors in this book certainly are mine.

Rongxing Guo
June 2010

NOTES FROM THE AUTHOR

- The geographical scope of the Chinese economy covers only mainland China, although Hong Kong, Macau, and Taiwan are mentioned in a number of the chapters.
- Chinese names are customarily written in the order of family name (which is in the single syllable in most cases) followed by the given name.
- Chinese names and geographic terms in mainland China are written in China's official (*pinyin*) form, while those outside mainland China are in the conventional form.
- Unless stated otherwise, the statistical data used in this book are from China statistical yearbooks (NBS, all issues).
- For the sake of convenience, specific autonomous regions and municipalities directly under the central government are referred to alongside provinces by a single name.
- The unit of the Chinese currency (RMB) is yuan (¥). The official exchange rates and the estimated PPP rates of the RMB to the US dollar are shown on the next page.

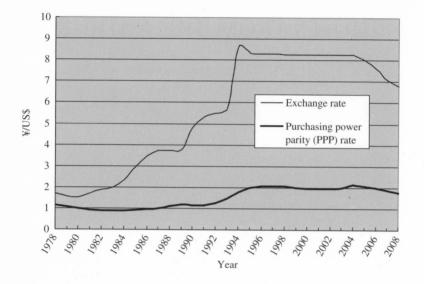

CHAPTER ONE

A BRIEF HISTORY OF CHINA

The "Mother River" monument in Lanzhou, Gansu province

The Yellow River (*Huanghe*) originates at the foot of the Kunlun mountains in the west and flows over 5,000 kilometers eastward to the Pacific Ocean. The river has been generally regarded as the cradle of the Chinese nation. It was along the banks of the river that the Chinese civilization first flowered. The geographical and hydrological characteristics of the Yellow River have shaped the Chinese nation, its 5,000-year civilization, as well as its distinctive philosophy and history . . .

Tao proliferates One;
(dao sheng yi)
One gives birth to Two;
(yi sheng er)
Two begets Three;
(er sheng san)
Three creates the world.
(san sheng wanwu)
                              —*Laozi (c.* 600 BC)

THE ORIGINS OF THE NATION

China, shaped like a rooster, and situated in East Asia, has a 14,500 km coastline along the East China Sea, the Korean Bay, the Yellow Sea, and the South China Sea. It has shared confines of approximately 22,140 km with North Korea, Russia, and Mongolia in the northeast and north; Kazakhstan, Kyrgyzstan, Tajikistan, Afghanistan, and Pakistan in the west; India and Nepal in the southwest; and Myanmar, Laos, and Vietnam in the south. During its thousands of years of history, there have been many legendary stories about this large nation, as well as its people, culture, and history.

In the prehistoric period, the progenitors of the Chinese people were scattered in small tribes over the middle reaches of the Yellow River. The present-day Chinese see themselves as the descendants of the Hua-Xia people. The Hua people, who first settled around Mt Hua near the middle reaches of the Yellow River Valley, together with the Xia people, who established themselves near the Xia River (the upper course of the Han River, a tributary of the Yangtze River), were referred to as the Hua-Xia people. Both of these areas were located in the central southern region of Shaanxi province. Toward the end of the Neolithic period, these tribes were already using a primitive form of writing, and had developed a system to measure time and to count numbers. They had also developed a variety of articles for daily use, including clothing, houses, weapons, pottery, and money.

According to mythology, the Chinese nation begins with *Pangu*, the creator of the universe. However, Chinese culture began to develop with the emergence of Emperor Yan (Yandi) and Emperor Huang (Huangdi) around 2300 BC. For this reason the Chinese today refer to themselves as the *yanhuang zisun* (the descendants of emperors Yan and Huang). During the period of the reign of Emperor Yan, Emperor Huang, and their successors, people were taught to observe "five basic relationships," including "good relations between sovereign and minister, father and son, husband and wife, elder brother and yonger brother, and friend and friend." This code of conduct, which was later developed systematically by Confucius (551–475 BC) and his disciples, established an ethical philosophy that has influenced Chinese society for the past 2,000 years.

From the twenty-first to the second century BC, three ancient dynasties—Xia, Shang, and Zhou—were established in the Yellow River Valley. The Xia dynasty, founded by the great Yu and his son, Qi, lasted until the sixteenth century BC. At the very least, the Xia dynasty marked an evolutionary stage between the late Neolithic cultures and the characteristic Chinese urban civilization of the Shang dynasty. During this period, the territorial boundaries of the Chinese nation began to take shape. The country was divided into nine administrative prefectures and a system of land taxes was established.

The Shang dynasty lasted from the sixteenth century BC to *c.* 1046 BC. The Shang dynasty (which was also called the Yin dynasty in its later stages) was founded by a rebel leader, Tang, who overthrew the last of the Xia rulers. Its civilization was based on agriculture, augmented by hunting and animal husbandry. Two of the most important events of the period were the development of a writing system, as revealed in archaic Chinese inscriptions found on tortoise shells and flat cattle bones (commonly called oracle bones), and the use of bronze metallurgy. A number of ceremonial bronze vessels with inscriptions date from the Shang period; the workmanship on the bronzes attests to a high level of civilization. For example, in the ruins of the city of Anyang (located at northern Henan province), the last capital of the Shang dynasty, archaeologists have unearthed over 150,000 pieces of oracle bones and other relics of the dynasty, suggesting that China experienced relative stability and prosperity in that period.

In a war with the 28th ruler of the Shang dynasty, the allied forces, under the command of King Wu, defeated the Shang army, leading to the foundation of a new dynasty named Zhou. The power of the rulers in the Zhou dynasty was based on *Zhongfa*—a system of inheritance and ancestral worship at a time when polygamy was the customary practice among the royalty and nobility.[1] In this way, a huge structure was built up, radiating from a central hub through endless feudal and in-feudal systems. Particularly noteworthy is that during the dynasty, education was widespread with a national university in the capital and various grades of schools. Scholars and intellectuals were held in high esteem and art and learning flourished as never before.

The Chinese name *zhongguo* (or "China" as called in the Western Hemisphere) derives from the term "center under heaven," a term that was first coined by King Wu of the Zhou dynasty. The king's intention was to move the Zhou capital from Haojing in western China to Luoyi (now known as Luoyang) in central China in order to maintain more effective control over the entire nation. During the second half of the Zhou dynasty (also known as the "Spring and Autumn and Warring States" period), a new group of regional rulers sought to obtain the services of talented individuals who could help to increase their political influence. The result was an unprecedented development of independent thinking and of original philosophies. The most celebrated philosophers of this period were Laozi, Confucius, Zhuangzi, Mencius, Mozi, Hanfei, and Xunzi. These individuals became the leading spirits of the Taoist, Confucian, Mohist, and Legalist schools of thought.

RISE AND FALL OF THE EMPIRE

In 221 BC, China was unified by Ying Zheng (also called Qin Shihuang), the first emperor of the Qin dynasty. The most important contribution of the Qin dynasty was the foundation of a completely new social and political order under a strict system of rewards and punishment favored by a group of scholars known as Legalists. In place of feudalism, the country was reorganized into 36 prefectures and a number of counties. Under this prefecture–county administration, all authority was vested in the central government. For the first time in history, China's written language, currency, and weights and measures were all unified and standardized. In order to consolidate and strengthen his imperial rule, the Emperor Qin Shihuang undertook large-scale construction projects, including national roadways, waterways, and a great wall that was 5,000 kilometers long. At its greatest extent, the Great Wall reaches from eastern Liaoning to northwestern Gansu. These activities required enormous levies of manpower and resources, not to mention repressive measures. After the conquest of the "barbarians" in the south, the Chinese territory was extended to the shores of the South China Sea. In spite of many political and military achievements, the multicultural development was monopolized in the Qin dynasty. Excessive trust was placed in the efficacy of the Legalist method, while the books on Confucianism and other schools of thought were burned in order to keep the people in a state of ignorance. Even worse, those intellectuals and scholars who criticized the government were either executed or forced to work as slave laborers. Due to its cruel and despotic rule, the Qin dynasty was to be overthrown less than 20 years after its triumph. The imperial system initiated during the Qin dynasty, however, set a pattern that was to be repeated over the next two millennia.

Five years later, Liu Bang reunited China and established a long-lived dynasty, the Han (206 BC–AD 220). Strong military forces made it possible for the Han dynasty to expand China's territories to the Western Dominion in today's Xinjiang and Central Asia, and also to Taiwan island in the East China Sea. The Han dynasty was a glorious age in Chinese history. The political institutions of the Qin and the Han dynasties were typical of all the dynasties that were to follow. The nine-chapter legal code drawn up in the early days of the Han served as a model for all later versions of Chinese codes. The political and military might of the Han dynasty was so impressive that since this time the Chinese have referred to themselves as the "Han" people. Under the Han rulers Confucianism was given special emphasis and those doing research on Confucian studies were given priority for public positions. Emperor Wudi (who reigned between 140–87 BC) listed the Confucian classics as subjects of study for his ministers, and appointed well-read scholars to positions of authority labeled *Boshi* (doctor). Confucianism thus gained official sanction over competing philo-sophical schools and became the core of Chinese culture. The Han period also produced China's most famous historian, Sima Qian (145–87 BC), whose *Shiji* (historical records) provides a detailed chronicle from the time of a legendary Huang emperor to the period of Emperor Wudi of the Han. This period was also marked by a series of technological advances, including two of the great Chinese inven-tions, paper and porcelain.

At the end of the Eastern Han period (AD 25–220)[2] political corruption and social chaos, together with widespread civil dis-turbances and royal throne usurpation, led eventually to the creation of three independent kingdoms—the Wei (AD 220–265) in the north, the Shu (AD 221–263) in the southwest, and the Wu (AD 222–280) in the southeast. China remained divided until AD 265 when the Jin dynasty was founded in Luoyang in central China. The Jin was not as militarily strong as the non-Han counterparts in the north, which encouraged the southward move of its capital to what is now called Nanjing (southern capital). Large-scale migration from the north to the south led to the Yangtze River Valley becoming more prosperous than ever before, and the economic and cultural center therefore shifted gradually to the southeast of the country. This transfer of the capital coincided with China's political fragmentation into a succession of dynasties that lasted from AD 420 to 589. In the Yellow River Valley, the non-Han peoples lived with the indigenous Han people, forming a more diverse and dynamic Chinese nation than ever before. Despite the political disunity of the times, there were notable technological advan-ces, including the invention of gunpowder and the wheelbarrow.

During this period, Buddhism achieved an increasing popularity in both northern and southern China.

China was reunified during the Sui dynasty (AD 581–618). The Sui is famous for its construction of the Grand Canal, which linked the Yellow River and the Huai and Yangtze rivers in order to secure improved communication between the south and the north of the country. In terms of human costs, only the Great Wall—which was constructed during the Qin dynasty—is comparable with the Canal. Like the Qin, the Sui was also a short-lived dynasty, which was succeeded by a powerful dynasty, the Tang (AD 618–907). The Tang period was the golden age of literature and art. A government system supported by a large class of Confucian literati selected through a system of civil service examinations was perfected under Tang rule. This competitive procedure was designed to draw the best talents into government. But perhaps an even greater consideration for the Tang rulers, aware that imperial dependence on powerful aristocratic families and warlords would have destabilizing consequences, was to create a body of career officials that had no autonomous territorial or functional power base. As it turned out, these scholar-officials acquired considerable status within their local communities, family ties, and shared values that connected them to the imperial court. From the Tang times until the closing days of the Qing empire in AD 1911, scholar-officials functioned often as intermediaries between the grassroots level and the government.

By the middle of the eighth century, Tang power had ebbed. Domestic economic instability and military defeat in AD 751 by Arabs at Talas, in Central Asia, marked the beginning of five centuries of steady military decline for the Chinese empire. Misrule, court intrigues, economic exploitation, and popular rebellions weakened the empire, making it possible for northern invaders to terminate the dynasty in AD 907. The next half-century saw the gradual fragmentation of China into Five Dynasties and Ten Kingdoms (AD 907–960).

In AD 960, China was reunited once again. The founders of the Song dynasty built an effective centralized bureaucracy staffed with civilian scholar-officials. Regional military governors and their supporters were replaced by centrally appointed officials. This system of civilian rule led to a greater concentration of power in the hands of the emperor and his palace bureaucracy than had been achieved in the previous dynasties. Unlike the Tang dynasty, the Song dynasty (AD 960–1279) was militarily confronted by powerful enemies from the north. The conflict between the Song and the Liao (a non-Han dynasty in northern China from AD 907 to 1125) lasted for more than a century before another non-Han dynasty, the Jin (AD 1115–1234), first defeated the Liao and then in 1127 took control of the Song's capital, Kaifeng, and captured two Song emperors as hostages. With northern China falling into the hands of the Jin, the Song capital moved from the Yellow River Valley to Lin'an (today's Hangzhou). As a result, the economic and cultural centers shifted from the central to the southeastern areas of China. Despite its military weakness, the Song dynasty contributed a great deal to the civilization of the world. Many Chinese inventions, including the compass, gunpowder, and movable-type printing, were introduced to the West during this period. Culturally, the Song also refined many of the developments of previous centuries. The Neo-Confucian philosophers found certain purity in the originality of the ancient classical texts of Confucianism. The most influential of these philosophers was Zhu Xi (AD 1130–1200), whose synthesis of Confucian thought and Buddhist, Taoist, and other ideas became the official imperial ideology from late Song times to the late nineteenth century. Neo-Confucian doctrines also came to play a dominant role in the intellectual life of Korea, Vietnam, and Japan.

In AD 1279 the Mongol cavalry, under the leadership of Genghis Khan, controlled the entire Chinese territory. The 88-year Yuan dynasty was an extraordinary one. Under Mongol rule, China once again expanded its borders. During the strongest period of the Yuan dynasty, China's territory even extended as far as the eastern part of Europe. The Mongols' extensive West Asian and European contacts led to a substantial degree of cultural exchange. This led to the development of rich cultural diversities. Western musical instruments were introduced and helped to enrich the Chinese performing arts. From this period dates the conversion to Islam, by Muslims from Central Asia, of growing numbers of Chinese in the northwest and southwest. Nestorianism and Roman Catholicism also enjoyed a period of toleration. Tibetan Buddhism (Lamaism) flourished, although native Taoism endured Mongol persecutions. Confucian governmental practices and examinations based on the Classics, which had fallen into disuse in north China during the period of disunity, were reinstated by the Mongols in the hope of maintaining order over Han society. Certain key Chinese innovations, such as porcelain production, playing cards, and medical literature, were introduced in Europe, while the production of thin glass and *cloisonné* became increasingly popular in China. European people were also enthralled by the account given by Venetian Marco Polo of his trip to "Cambaluc," the Great Khan's capital (now Beijing), and of the ways of life he encountered there.

In internal affairs, however, the Mongolian caste system—in which the majority of the Han people were seen as inferior to non-Han peoples—was not ideal. Widespread famines, resulting from natural disasters, political corruption, and misgovernment, eventually resulted in a successful anti-Mongol revolution led by Zhu Yuanzhang, who founded the Han-based dynasty, the Ming (AD 1368–1644) in Nanjing. In 1421, the Ming dynasty moved its seat to Beijing, after defeating the nomadic tribes of the northern part of the Great Wall. In Southeast Asia the Chinese armies reconquered Annam, as northern Vietnam was then known, and they also repelled the Mongols, while the Chinese fleet sailed the China seas and the Indian Ocean, venturing even as far as the east coast of Africa. The maritime Asian nations sent envoys with tribute for the Chinese emperor. The maritime expeditions stopped suddenly after 1433, probably as the result of the great expense of large-scale expeditions at a time of preoccupation with securing northern borders against the threat from the Mongols. Pressure from the powerful Neo-Confucian bureaucracy led to a revival of a society that was centered on agriculture. Internally, the Grand Canal was expanded to its farthest limits and proved to be a stimulus to domestic trade. The stability of the Ming dynasty, which suffered no major disruptions of the population (then around 100 million), economy, arts, society, and politics, promoted a belief among the Chinese that they had achieved the most satisfactory civilization on earth and that nothing foreign was either needed or welcome.

As the Ming dynasty declined, China's last, also the last minority-based dynasty, the Qing (AD 1644–1911), was set up by the Manchus, who rose to power in Manchuria (today's northeast part of China). Compared with the Mongols, the period of Manchu rule over China can be viewed as successful. At the height of the Qing dynasty, the Manchus utilized the best minds and richest human resources of the nation, regardless of race. Although the Manchus were not Han Chinese and were subjected to strong resistance, especially in the south, they had assimilated a great deal of the Han-Chinese culture before conquering China proper. Realizing that in order to dominate the empire they would have to do things in the Chinese manner, the Manchus retained many institutions of Ming and earlier Chinese derivation. Furthermore, the Han-based political ideologies and cultural traditions of the Chinese were adopted by the Manchus, resulting in virtually total cultural assimilation of the Manchus by the Han Chinese. After the subduing of China proper, the Manchus conquered Outer Mongolia (now the Mongolian People's Republic) in the late seventeenth century. In the eighteenth century they gained control of Central Asia as far as the Pamir Mountains and established a protectorate over Tibet. The Qing thus became the first dynasty to eliminate successfully all danger to China proper from across its land borders. Under the rule of the Manchu dynasty the empire grew once again; during this period Taiwan, the last outpost of anti-Manchu resistance, was incorporated into China for the first time. In addition, the Qing emperors received tribute from many neighboring states.

The 1840s marked a turning point in Chinese history. In the early nineteenth century Britain was smuggling large quantities of opium into China, causing a substantial outflow of Chinese silver and grave economic disruption. In an effort to protect its opium trade, in 1840 Britain initiated the First Opium War. The war ended in 1842, after the Qing court signed the Treaty of Nanjing with Britain, bartering away China's national sovereignty. Subsequently, China declined into a semi-colonial and semi-feudal country. After the Opium War, Britain and other Western powers, including Belgium, the Netherlands, Prussia, Spain, Portugal, the United States (US), and France, seized "concessions" and divided China into "spheres of influence." The second half of the nineteenth century saw the emergence of many peasant leaders and national heroes. The Revolution of 1911, led by Dr Sun Yatsen, is of great significance in modern Chinese history, since with the founding of the Republic of China (ROC) it discarded the feudal monarchical system that had ruled China for more than 2,000 years. In the following decades, however, the Chinese nation was on the edge of bankruptcy.[3]

CHINA IN THE NEW MILLENNIUM

During the past century, China's economic development had been interrupted on a number of separate occasions. The Chinese economy was nearly bankrupt at the end of the Civil War in the late 1940s, and was seriously damaged by both the Great Leap Forward (1958–60) and the Cultural Revolution (1966–76) movements. However, since the late 1970s, when the Chinese government began the gradual transformation of its Stalinesque centrally planned system, the Chinese economy has grown extremely rapidly. In the reform era since 1978, China has been one of the world's fastest growing economies. Between 1978 and 2008, China's real GDP grew at an average annual rate of almost 10 percent.

With China achieving vigorous economic growth since the implementation of market-oriented reform in the late 1970s (see Figure 1.1), the Chinese model has been generally regarded as having achieved the most successful transformation of all of the former Soviet-type economies in terms of the improvement of economic performance. However, it should also be noted that China still lags behind many market-based, industrialized economies. The per capita income of China has still been

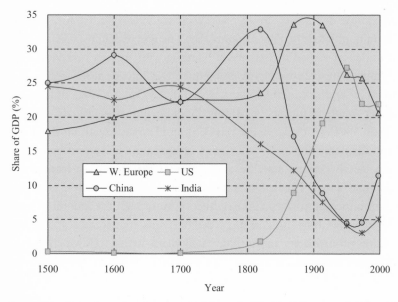

Source: Created by the author, based on Maddison, A. *The World Economy: A Millennial Perspective.* Paris: OECD Development Center, 2001.

Figure 1.1   A dynamic view of the Chinese economy, AD 1500–2000

much lower than that of the US, Japan, and other newly industrialized economies. While China's over-centralized planning system was largely responsible for its poor socioeconomic performance, there were also historical, social, and cultural factors that hindered its socioeconomic development. Indeed, it is not easy to develop a market-system framework within a short period of time in China—a huge country utilizing the centrally planned system for nearly 30 years and that was, in particular, deeply influenced by long periods of feudalism but rarely by economic democracy.

Over recent decades, the Chinese economy has experienced dramatic changes and a more rapid development than many other transitional centrally planned economies (CPEs). This was the result of a combination of both internal and external circumstances. In these first few years of the twenty-first century, we can see that China is scheduled to develop its economy along its own distinctive lines. At the same time, China's current situation poses many significant challenges to its economy. Many inherent problems in relation to economic development still persist. If the Chinese government does not address these properly, its efforts, based on the successful introduction of Chinese-style reforms, will inevitably be jeopardized.

More than 2,000 years ago, Confucius used to instruct his pupils through the telling of this autobiographical story: "Since the age of 15, I have devoted myself to learning; since 30, I have been well established; since 40, I have understood many things and have no longer been confused; since 50, I have known my heaven-sent duty; since 60, I have been able to distinguish right and wrong in other people's words; and since 70, I have been able to do what I intended freely without breaking the rules." Hopefully, after the celebration of the 60th anniversary of the PRC, the Chinese leaders will finally be emerging from their past confused age and know where to go and what to do next.

ENDNOTES

1 According to the *Zhongfa* system, the eldest son born of the highest-ranking wife of a member of the royal household or nobility was called the "major branch" and inherited the right of succession to his father's throne or noble title. Other son(s) was (were) known as "minor branch(es)."

2 Historically, the Han dynasty is divided into two periods: the Western Han had its capital in Chang'an in the west; while the Eastern Han had its capital in Luoyang in the east.

3 The major events that occurred in Chinese society during the twentieth century are listed below in chronological order: 1912, China's final dynasty, the Qing, was replaced by the Republic of China (ROC); 1937, Japan invaded China and the War of Resistance against Japan began; 1945, Japan surrendered unconditionally and, thereafter, the Civil War between the Nationalists and the Communists broke out; 1949, the People's Republic of China (PRC) was founded, followed by the large-scale land reform and socialist transformation.

CHAPTER TWO

SPATIAL AND ADMINISTRATIVE DIVISIONS

The Great Wall, northern Beijing
Copyright © Rongxing Guo

In any discussion of the Chinese economy, at least two important points must be noted: first, China's vast territorial size and the diversity of physical environments and natural resource endowments have inevitably resulted in considerable regional economic differences; second, China has a population of more than 1.3 billion, comprised of 56 ethnic groups. In short, the Chinese economy is one of the most complicated and diversified spatial systems to be found anywhere in the world. The only feasible approach one can adopt is, therefore, to divide it into smaller geographic elements through which one can gain a better insight into the spatial mechanisms and regional characteristics.

> Each block of land should be divided into nine plots, the whole containing 900 *mu*. The central plot will be the public field and the eight households, each owning 100 *mu* farm, will collaborate in cultivating the public field. Not until the public land has been properly attended to, may each household attend to its private plot. This is how the countrymen should be required to learn.
>
> —*Mencius* (372–289 BC)

ADMINISTRATIVE DIVISIONS

At present, China's territorial-administrative hierarchy has three different types of provincial-level units: *sheng* (province), *zhizhiqu* (autonomous regions) and *zhixiashi* (municipalities directly under the central government). In the Chinese state administration "autonomous" refers to self-government by a large and single (but not necessarily majority) ethnic minority in any given unit within the territorial hierarchy. Autonomous regions are provincial-level units of state administration where the presence of an ethnic minority is officially recognized. They have the name of the specific ethnic minority incorporated in their title, as, for example, in the Guangxi Zhuang autonomous region, where Guangxi is the geographic name of the region and the Zhuang is the name of a nationality. Municipalities are large cities, directly subordinate to the Chinese Communist Party Central Committee (CCPCC) and the State Council.

It should be noted that the three kinds of provincial administrations (*sheng*, *zizhiqu*, and *zhixiashi*) have different functions. More often than not, top *zhixiashi* leaders have been appointed as members of the Politburo of the CCPCC, something that has only happened to a small number of *sheng* and *zizhiqu* leaders. The autonomous regions (*zizhiqu*) are only established in areas where the ethnic minorities consist of the major portion of population. Compared to other forms of provincial administrations, the *zizhiqu* is, at least in form, the most politically and culturally autonomous of the three kinds of provincial administrations. In addition, Hong Kong and Macau—which returned to China in 1997 and 1999, respectively—are now China's two special administrative regions (SARs). It was agreed on handover that the existing political and economic systems that prevailed prior to these dates would be maintained for 50 years.

While the formation of most provinces had taken place well before the founding of the PRC, in recent decades a few of the others were either incorporated into their neighboring provinces or divided into new provinces. For example, in 1954, Pingyuan province, which included the marginal administrative areas of present Hebei, Shanxi, Shandong, and Henan provinces, was abolished. In 1988, Hainan Island, Guangdong province, was established as a new province; and, in 1997, Chongqing city and its surrounding areas, all of which had belonged to Sichuan province, became a province-level municipality under the direct control of the central government. In addition, during the history of the PRC, some provincially marginal areas have been administratively transposed between the neighboring provinces. For example, in 1953, Xuzhou administrative region, Shandong province, was placed under the administration of Jiangsu province; and, in 1955, Yutai county was transferred from Anhui to Jiangsu provinces.

There are three classes of administrative divisions in China. The first-class administrative divisions include provinces, autonomous regions, and municipalities directly under the central government. The second-class administrative divisions refer to prefectures, autonomous prefectures, municipalities, and other prefecture-level administrative divisions. The third-class administrative divisions relate to counties, autonomous counties, and other county-level administrative divisions. An organizational pattern involving more classes of administrative divisions has been generally known to have a lower level of administrative efficiency. Recently, some provinces have been granted permission by the central government to practice a two-class pattern of administrative division (that is, to eliminate the second-class administrative divisions) in order to increase spatial economic efficiency. However, this administrative reform has encountered difficulties in dealing with large provinces. For example, in Henan or Shandong province there are more than 100 counties and county-level administrative divisions. Without the participation of the prefecture-level administrations, it would be very difficult, if not impossible, for a provincial governor to exert any direct effective influence on all of these county magistrates concurrently.

Most of China's provinces, autonomous regions, and municipalities that are under the direct control of the central government,[1] which are the average size and scale of a European country in population and land area, are considerable political and economic systems in their own right (see Table 2.1). These large provincial administrations, although have some comparative advantages over the small ones in some circumstances, have been known to lack spatial administrative efficiency. Given China's huge size and enormous population,

Table 2.1 China's Current Provincial Conditions (2008)[1]

Province	Capital City	Political Form[2]	Population (Million Persons)	Land Area (000 km^2)
Anhui	Hefei	S	63.3	130.0
Beijing	Beijing	ZXS	13.8	16.8
Chongqing	Chongqing	ZXS	31.0	82.4
Fujian	Fuzhou	S	34.4	120.0
Gansu	Lanzhou	S	25.8	390.0
Guangdong	Guangzhou	S	77.8	180.0
Guangxi	Liuzhou	ZZQ	47.9	230.0
Guizhou	Guiyang	S	38.0	170.0
Hainan	Haikou	S	8.0	34.0
Hebei	Shijiazhuang	S	67.0	190.0
Heilongjiang	Harbin	S	38.1	460.0
Henan	Zhengzhou	S	95.6	160.0
Hubei	Wuhan	S	59.8	180.0

Table 2.1 (Continued)

Hunan	Changsha	S	66.0	210.0
Inner Mongolia	Huhehaot	ZZQ	23.8	1100.0
Jiangsu	Nanjing	S	73.6	100.0
Jiangxi	Nanchang	S	41.9	160.0
Jilin	Changchun	S	26.9	180.0
Liaoning	Shenyang	S	41.9	150.0
Ningxia	Yinchuan	ZZQ	5.6	66.0
Qinghai	Xi'ning	S	5.2	720.0
Shaanxi	Xi'an	S	36.6	190.0
Shandong	Ji'nan	S	90.4	150.0
Shanghai	Shanghai	ZXS	16.1	5.8
Shanxi	Taiyuan	S	32.7	150.0
Sichuan	Chengdu	S	86.4	477.6
Tianjin	Tianjin	ZXS	10.0	11.0
Tibet	Lasha	ZZQ	2.6	1200.0
Xinjiang	Wurumuqi	ZZQ	18.8	1600.0
Yunnan	Kunming	S	42.9	380.0
Zhejiang	Hanzhou	S	46.1	100.0

Notes
1 Hong Kong, Macau, and Taiwan are not included.
2 S (*sheng*) = province; ZZQ (*zizhiqu*) = autonomous region; ZXS (*zhixiashi*) = municipality directly under the central government.

establishing new provincial administrations (including provinces or other provincial-level units) in the border areas of some adjacent, large provinces seems to serve two positive functions. The first concerns the increase of the efficiency of spatial administration over the marginal, adjacent areas by transferring the multitude of administrative systems into a unitary administrative structure; and the second relates to the realization of increased economies of scale for provincial administration by separating the marginal areas out of the oversized provinces.

Over recent decades, the total number of China's provincial administrations has increased: from 29 in the mid-1950s to 30 in 1988 and 31 in 1997. But economic geographers and regional scientists still believe that the introduction of smaller provinces may help to improve the spatial efficiency of the Chinese economy. However, it seems unlikely that, under current political and economic systems, the central government will be able to deal with so many provincial administrations.

GREAT REGIONS

When the PRC was founded on October 1, 1949, the Chinese economy was managed through six great administrative regions (North, Northeast, East, Central South, Southwest, and Northwest). With the exception of the North region, which was under the administration of the central government, the other five great regions also had their own governmental bodies in charge of agriculture and forestry, industry, public finance, trade, and so on. In 1954, the six great administrative regions were abolished and, three years before their final reorganization in 1961, seven cooperative commissions were established in the North, Northeast, East, Central, South, Southwest, and Northwest regions. The six great regional administrations were destroyed during the Cultural Revolution period (1966–76). In 1970 the Chinese economy was spatially organized via 10 economic cooperative zones (namely, Southwest, Northwest, Center, South, East, Northeast, North, Shandong, Fujian and Jiangxi, and Xinjiang). It is generally believed that this arrangement was based on the centrally planned system and reflected the state's efforts to meet the desperate need for regional self-sufficiency at the high point of the Cold War era.

Since the early 1980s, China's official statistical authorities have used six great regions (as shown in Figure 2.1):

- North (including Beijing, Tianjin, Hebei, Shanxi, and Inner Mongolia, with 16.3 percent of the land area).
- Northeast (including Liaoning, Jilin, and Heilongjiang, with 8.2 percent of the land area).
- East (including Shanghai, Jiangsu, Zhejiang, Anhui, Fujian, Jiangxi, and Shandong, with 8.3 percent of the land area).

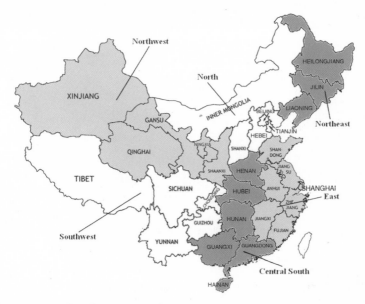

Figure 2.1 The six great regions

- Central South (including Henan, Hubei, Hunan, Guangdong, Guangxi, and Hainan, with 10.6 percent of the land area).
- Southwest (including Sichuan, Chongqing, Guizhou, Yunnan, and Tibet, with 24.6 percent of the land area).
- Northwest (including Shaanxi, Gansu, Qinghai, Ningxia, and Xinjiang, with 32.0 percent of the land area).

GEOGRAPHICAL BELTS

The 12 provinces surrounded by the Yellow, East China, and South China seas are classified as the coastal area, while the remaining provinces are regarded as the inland area (see Figure 2.2). Generally, the coastal area is more developed than the inland area, as a result of its proximity to the market economies along the western shore of the Pacific Ocean, as well as the fact that it was the region that experienced

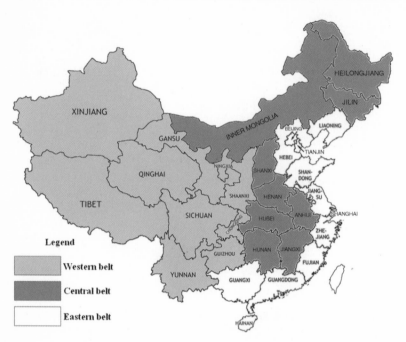

Figure 2.2   The Eastern, Central, and Western belts

the earlier introduction of economic reform and opening up to the outside world.

— Even though China's economic divergence has not been as large within the inland area as it has between the inland and coastal areas, there are still some plausible reasons to explain why the inland area needs to be further divided into smaller geographical units. As the western part of the inland area has less-developed social and economic infrastructures than the eastern part, China's inland area can be further divided into two sections—the Central belt, which is next to the coastal area (here it is referred as the Eastern belt), and the Western belt.

The Eastern, Central, and Western belts (shown in Figure 2.2) have their component provinces, as follows:

- Eastern belt (including Liaoning, Hebei, Beijing, Tianjin, Shandong, Jiangsu, Shanghai, Zhejiang, Fujian, Guangdong, Hainan, and Guangxi, with 13.5 percent of the land area).
- Central belt (including Shanxi, Jilin, Heilongjiang, Anhui, Henan, Hubei, Hunan, Jiangxi, and Inner Mongolia, with 29.8 percent of the land area).
- Western belt (including Sichuan, Chongqing, Guizhou, Yunnan, Shaanxi, Gansu, Qinghai, Tibet, Ningxia, and Xinjiang, with 56.7 percent of the land area).

SOUTHERN AND NORTHERN PARTS

The introduction of the concept of the "North" and "South" of China in this book seems to be necessary for the bi-regional comparison of the Chinese economy. From the south to the north, the land mass of China is characterized by dramatic geographical, geological, and hydro-geological diversities. Its land surface ascends from north to south in four distinct climate zones: the arid zone, the semi-arid zone, the semi-humid zone, and the humid zone.

In addition to the natural and climatic diversities, social and cultural conditions also differ between northern and southern China. Without good reason, the Chinese are usually identified as Northerners and Southerners in terms of their birthplaces and, occasionally, the homes of their parents or relatives when they are introduced to one another. While it is not quite clear when the saying "South China raises intelligent scholars while marshals mainly come from the North" was aired, and whether or not it can be used to spatially characterize China's ethnic nature, many conflicts and wars in Chinese history did take place in the Northern part.

The first major Han-Chinese migration from the northern to the southern part of the Yangtze River took place during the Wei (AD 220–265), the Jin (AD 265–420), and the South and North dynasties (AD 420–589), and was accelerated during the Five Dynasties and Ten Kingdoms period (AD 907–960) when China's northern part became the nation's battlefield. Large-scale Han-Chinese migration was promoted later by frequent wars between the Chinese and the Liao, Jin, Mongol, and other non-Han minorities in the North Song (AD 960–1126) and the South Song (AD 1127–1279) dynasties. In the wars with their far northern enemies, the Han-Chinese first lost their northern part after the late North Song dynasty. Naturally, the frequent wars greatly accelerated the emigration of northern intellectuals to the Southern part of the country.

The geographic definition of the Southern and Northern parts may differ slightly. For example, the Qinling Range and the Huaihe River are traditionally used to divide the South and North, while the Yangtze River is sometimes known as the boundary of northern and southern China. The only difference between the two definitions lies in the fact that the Qinling Range and the Huaihe River are located in Shaanxi, Henan, Anhui, and Jiangsu provinces, while the Yangtze River runs through Sichuan, Chongqing, Hubei, Anhui, Jiangsu, and Shanghai provinces. In most cases, nevertheless, there are about an equal number of provinces in each of the Northern and Southern parts, shown in Figure 2.3:

- Northern part (including Beijing, Tianjin, Hebei, Shanxi, Inner Mongolia, Liaoning, Jilin, Heilongjiang, Shaanxi, Gansu, Qinghai, Ningxia, Xinjiang, Shandong, and Henan, with 59.8 percent of the land area).
- Southern belt (including Shanghai, Jiangsu, Zhejiang, Anhui, Fujian, Jiangxi, Sichuan, Chongqing, Guizhou, Yunnan, Tibet, Hubei, Hunan, Guangdong, Guangxi, and Hainan, with 40.2 percent of the land area).

ETHNO-CULTURAL AREAS

China is not a culturally and ethnically homogeneous country. In addition to the Han majority, 55 other ethnic minorities also exist in China.[2] In 1947 China's first, and ethnically based, autonomous region, Inner Mongolia, was established at the provincial level by the CCP.

Figure 2.3   The Northern and Southern parts

Then, after the founding of the PRC in 1949, the Chinese government began to introduce a system of regional autonomy for other non-Han ethnic areas. In 1952, the Chinese government issued the Program for the Implementation of Regional Ethnic Autonomy of the People's Republic of China, which included provisions on the establishment of ethnic autonomous areas and the composition of organs of self-government, as well as the right of self-government for such organs. The first National People's Congress (NPC), convened in 1954, included the system of regional autonomy for ethnic minorities in the Consti-tution of the PRC. Thereafter, four autonomous regions appeared in China: They are Xinjiang Uygur autonomous region (October 1955), Guangxi Zhuang autonomous region (March 1958), Ningxia Hui autonomous region (October 1958), and Tibet autonomous region (September 1965).

In most cases, the name of an ethnic autonomous area consists of the name of the place, the name of the ethnic group, and the character indicating the administrative status, in that order. Take the Ningxia Hui autonomous region as an example: "Ningxia" is the name of the place, "Hui" is the name of the ethnic group, and "region" indicates the level of administration. By the end of 2005, China's non-Han ethnic administrative areas included:

(1) five autonomous regions including:

- Guangxi Zhuang autonomous region
- Inner Mongolia autonomous region
- Ningxia Hui autonomous region
- Tibet autonomous region
- Xinjiang Uygur autonomous region

(2) 30 autonomous prefectures (APs) in nine provincial administrations including:

- Gansu province: Gannan Tibetan AP; Linxia Hui AP
- Guizou province: Qiandongnan Miao-Dong AP; Qiannan Buyi-Miao AP; Qianxi'nan Buyi-Miao AP
- Hubei province: Enshi Tujia-Miao AP
- Hunan province: Xiangxi Tujia-Miao AP
- Jilin province: Yanbian Korean AP
- Qinghai province: Yushu Tibetan AP; Hainan Tibetan AP; Huangnan Tibetan AP; Haibei Tibetan AP; Guoluo Tibetan AP; Haixi Mongolian–Tibetan AP
- Sichuan province: Ganzi Tibetan AP; Liangshan Yi AP; A'ba Tibetan-Qiang AP
- Xinjiang Uygur autonomous region: Bayin'guole Mongolian AP; Bo'ertala Mongolian AP; Kezilesu Kirgiz AP; Changji Hui AP; Yili Kazak AP
- Yunnan province: Xishuangbanna Dai AP; Dehong Dai-Jingpo AP; Nujiang Lisu; Dali Bai AP; Diqing Tibetan AP; Honghe Hani-Yi AP; Wenshan Zhuang-Miao AP; Chuxiong Yi AP

Figure 2.4 The ethno-culture areas

and (3) 119 county-level autonomous administrations in 18 provincial administrations (see Figure 2.4).[3]

Communities of one ethnic group may establish, according to their respective sizes, different autonomous administrations. If we take the Hui ethnic group as an example, this includes: (1) a provincial administration, called Ningxia Hui autonomous region; (2) a sub-provincial administration, called the Linxia Hui autonomous prefecture of Gansu province; and (3) a sub-prefecture administration, called the Mengcun Hui autonomous county of Hebei province. In places where different ethnic groups live, each autonomous administration can be established based on either one ethnic group (such as the Tibet autonomous region, Liangshan Yi autonomous prefecture of Sichuan province, and Jingning She autonomous county of Zhejiang province); or two or more ethnic groups (such as Haixi Mongolian-Tibetan autonomous prefecture of Qinghai province, and Jishishan Bao'nan-Dongxiang-Salar autonomous county of Gansu province). If a minority ethnic group lives in an autonomous area of a bigger ethnic group, the former may establish its own subordinate autonomous areas. For example, Yili Kazak autonomous prefecture and Yanqi Hui autonomous county are both to be found in the Xinjiang Uygur autonomous region.

Organizationally, China's non-Han ethnic administrative areas are oriented in a multi-ethnic manner. For example, in addition to deputies from the ethnic group or groups exercising regional autonomy in the area concerned, the people's congresses of the autonomous areas also include an appropriate number of members from other ethnic groups who live in that autonomous area. Among the chairman or vice-chairmen of the standing committee of the people's congress of an autonomous area there shall be one or more citizens of the ethnic group or groups exercising regional autonomy in the area concerned. The head of an autonomous region, autonomous prefecture, or autonomous county alike shall be a citizen of the ethnic group exercising regional autonomy in the area concerned. Other members of the people's governments of the autonomous areas shall include an appropriate number of members of the ethnic group exercising regional autonomy alongside members of other ethnic minorities. The functionaries of the working departments subsidiary to the organs of self-government shall be composed in a similar fashion.

ENDNOTES

1   In what follows, unless stated otherwise, we will use the term "province" to denote all of the three kinds of administrative divisions.
2   As of 2008, the largest ethnic minorities include Zhuang (16 million people), Manchu (10 million), Hui (9 million), Miao (7.6 million), Uygur (7.5 million), and Yi (7 million)—NBS (2009).
3   More detailed information about all these county-level autonomous administrations can be found in the official website of China Ethnic Museum <www.cnmuseum.com>.

CHAPTER THREE

THE FOUNDATION OF THE CHINESE ECONOMY (I)

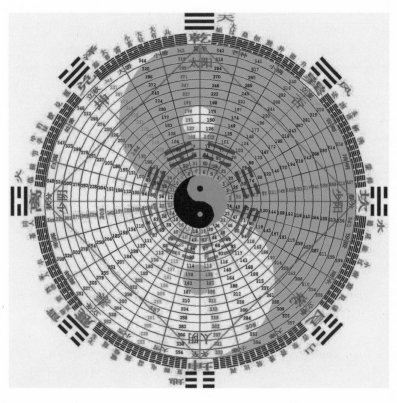

Bagua map

Bagua (literally "eight symbols") represents a range of interrelated concepts of nature in ancient China. Each symbol consists of three lines; and each line is either unbroken (labeled as "—") or broken (labeled as "– –"), representing *yang* or *yin*, respectively. The trigrams have correspondences in astronomy, astrology, geography, geomancy, and other natural characteristics as follows:

Symbol	Name	Nature	Direction	Extended Meaning
☰	Qián	Heaven	South	Expansive energy, the sky
☴	Xùn	Wind	Southwest	Gentle penetration, flexibility
☵	Kǎn	Water	West	Danger, rapid rivers, the abyss, the moon
☶	Gèn	Mountain	Northwest	Stillness, immovability
☷	Kūn	Earth	North	Receptive energy, that which yields
☳	Zhèn	Thunder	Northeast	Excitation, revolution, division
☲	Lí	Fire	East	Rapid movement, radiance, the sun
☱	Duì	Lake	Southeast	Joy, satisfaction, stagnation

> *When a seed is planted in spring*
> (chun zhong yi li su)
> *There are thousands of grains harvested in the fall.*
> (qiu shou wan ke li)
> *While all land across the country has been cultivated*
> (si hai wu xian tian)
> *Why do farmers still die from starvation?*
> (nong fu you e si)
> —*Minnong* (*Li Shen*, AD 772–846)

LAND AND WATER

China's vast size, which is comparable to that of the US or Canada, means that it possesses an abundance of natural resources. For example, China's cropland accounts for nearly 7 percent of the world total, making it the fourth largest (after Russia, the US, and India); China has 9 percent of the world's total permanent pasture (exceeded only by Australia and Russia); and more than 3 percent of the world's forestland and woodland (after Russia, Brazil, Canada, and the US). However, if population size is taken into account, China's natural resources are not richer than the world as a whole. For instance, China's per capita cultivated land area is less than one-third the world's; its per capita forestland and woodland is approximately one-seventh of the world's.

China has provided sustenance and other basic necessities for one-fifth of the world's population, although it has only 7 percent of the world's cultivated land. China is now an important consumer of agricultural commodities, leading the world in the consumption of wheat, rice, cotton, palm oil, and rubber. The US or India is ranked first or second in terms of the consumption of maize, soybeans, soy oil, sugar, and tea, but China is usually in the second or third place. It is noteworthy that this kind of development pattern has created many serious environmental problems that are the result of inappropriate policies and approaches in agricultural production. During the 1960s and 1970s, the Chinese government saw "taking grain production as the key link" (*yi liang wei gang*) in order to maximize self-sufficiency in the supply of foodstuffs. This policy has been generally known to ignore the comparative advantages between the regions differing in natural conditions, and accelerated the conversion of forestland, wetland, and marginal land into cropland.

The land mass of China is characterized by dramatic geographical, geological, and hydrogeological diversities. Its land surface ascends from north to south in four distinct zones: arid zone, semi-arid zone, semi-humid zone, and humid zone. The climate ranges from the tropical zone in the south to the frigid zone in the north, and from the arid and semi-arid zones in the northwest to the humid and semi-humid zones in the southeast. As a result, the regional distribution of natural resources is extremely unequal in China. In general, the agricultural and biological resources diminish from the south to the north and from the east to the west. In addition, monthly precipitation has been rather uneven in both southern (such as Guangzhou and Shanghai) and northern (such as Beijing, Lanzhou, Shenyang, and Yinchuan) cities. Throughout China, rainfall usually occurs heavily in summer but not in winter. This is particularly so for cities in the northwest (such as Lanzhou and Yinchuan), where there is almost no rainfall during the seasons from October to May.

The precipitation is more than 1,000 mm/yr in the southern part and more than 1,600 mm/yr in the southern coastal area, while it only ranges between 100 and 800 mm/yr in the northern part. In particular, the Talimu, Tulufan, and Chaidamu basins in the Northwest region have less than 25 mm of precipitation per annum. As a result of the suitable climate and adequate rainfall, the southern part is the dominant rice producer; and wheat is the main foodstuff in the lower Yellow River Valley (such as Henan, Shandong, Hebei, northern Jiangsu, and Anhui provinces) and the area south of the Great Wall. A selection of top five agriculture-based provinces is shown below:

- Hunan, Sichuan, Jiangsu, Hubei, and Guangdong for rice
- Henan, Shandong, Jiangsu, Hebei, and Sichuan for wheat
- Shandong, Jilin, Hebei, Sichuan, and Henan for maize
- Heilongjiang, Henan, Jilin, Shandong, and Anhui for soybean
- Shandong, Hebei, Henan, Hubei, and Jiangsu for cotton
- Shandong, Sichuan, Anhui, Jiangsu, and Henan for rapeseeds
- Henan, Yunnan, Shandong, Guizhou, and Hunan for tobacco
- Zhejiang, Hunan, Sichuan, Anhui, and Fujian for tea
- Shandong, Hebei, Guangdong, Sichuan, and Liaoning for fruits.

China now faces almost all of the problems related to water resources that are faced by countries across the globe. China's rapid economic growth, industrialization, and urbanization have outpaced infrastructural investment and management capacity, and have created widespread problems of water scarcity. In the areas of the North China

Plain, where about half of China's wheat and corn is grown and there are extensive peach orchards, drought is an ever-looming threat. With one-fifth of the world's population, China has only 8 percent of the fresh water. China's annual renewable water reserves were about 2.8 trillion cubic meters, which ranked it fifth in the world, behind Brazil, Russia, Canada, and Indonesia, but ahead of the US. However, in terms of per capita availability of water reserves, China is one of the lowest in the world—barely one-quarter of the world average (WRI 2003). In the coming decades, China will be under severe water stress as defined by the international standard.

Large-scale underground water extraction began in the 1950s and has increased significantly over the course of the past 20 years. Accordingly, underground water use as a percentage of the total water supply has also increased. The over-exploitation of groundwater has led to a marked and continuous drawdown of underground water levels in China. From time to time deeper wells have to be installed. Recent surveys indicate that the cones of depression in the deep aquifers have joined together to form a huge inter-provincial cone of depression in the North China Plain. There is growing competition for water between communities, sectors of the economy, and individual provinces. There are already a dozen seawater desalination plants in China. China has also invested in a seawater desalination project to carry desalinated seawater to the Beijing municipality. However, the problem with respect to the wide utilization of the desalinated seawater in the vast rural area is the cost. Many farmers in China are still neither able nor willing to absorb such a high price, since, in traditional culture, the waters in rivers and lakes have been free of any such charge.

In addition to water scarcity for China as a whole, there is considerable unevenness in terms of the amount of water resources available in different regions of the country. In general, the northern part is poor in surface water, but modestly rich in groundwater in a few provinces, including Qinghai, Xinjiang, Inner Mongolia, and Heilongjiang. The southern part is water rich. The areas south of the Yangtze River, which account for only 37 percent of the country's total territory, have 81 percent of its total water resources. By contrast, the areas north of the Yangtze, which make up 63 percent of China's territory, possess only 19 percent of the country's total water resources (Chen and Cai 2000). As a result of the uneven distribution, the per capita water rate in northern China (especially the areas in the Liaohe River Valley in the northeast China and in the Haihe River Valley around Tianjin municipality) is much lower than that of the national average. Water shortage has become a major economic bottleneck to these areas.

China is plagued with unevenly distributed water and land resources: more water vis-à-vis less land in southern China and less water vis-à-vis more land in northern China. North China accounts for over one-third of the country's total population, nearly one half of cultivated land, but only one-eighth of the total water resources. Over 80 percent direct water runoff in China takes place in the south. The Haihe and Yellow river valleys have been stricken by chronic drought. Yet, further south, large amounts of water from the Yangtze empty into the sea each year. Today, water scarcity is often viewed as a major threat to China's long-term security. The degradation of underground water resources and the deterioration in the quality of underground water quality have become a striking environmental problem in many of China's cities.

Given the existence of surface water surplus in southern China and a freshwater shortage in northern China, is it feasible to transfer water from the water-rich south to the north? A water transfer project had been discussed for more than two decades before it was started on December 27, 2002. The South-North Water Diversion project involves the construction of three canals running 1,300 kilometers across the eastern, middle, and western parts of China, linking the country's four major rivers—the Yangtze, Yellow, Huaihe, and Haihe rivers. The gigantic project is expected to cost US$59 billion and to take 50 years to complete. If all goes well, the project will carry more than 40 billion tons of water annually from the Yangtze River basin to Beijing and to other provinces in northern China. However, this project cannot completely solve the water shortage problems in China.

MINERALS AND ENERGY RESOURCES

Two major characteristics define China: its population is huge and its economy has been growing very fast for at least three decades. Minerals and energy resources are the basic component among the factors that influence social and economic activities, especially for less-developed economies lacking capital and technology. Theoretically, in a nation whose manufacturing and other high-tech industries are not internationally competitive, one of the most feasible ways to eradicate poverty and backwardness is to develop the natural resource-based sectors. In recent decades, Chinese economic development has followed this path. Until recently, the natural resource-based sectors were still playing the most important role in the development of some less-developed areas.

China has become the world's major player in both output and input markets. The data on the total consumption of metals and energy products presented in Table 3.1 reinforce the importance of China in world consumption markets. In the areas of both metals and coal, China is always ranked first, with shares of between 15 percent and one-third of world consumption, and the US is ranked either second or third; in other energies, the US is first and China is second. Increasing commodity demand from the giants obviously supports prices, other things being equal, but prices also depend on supply. Most analysts hold that, in recent years, Chinese demand has increased the prices of most metals because the growth in supply has not kept pace with the growth in demand (Winters and Yusuf 2007, pp. 16–17).[1]

According to a report published by the World Resources Institute (WRI), China has 8.39 percent of the world's reserves of 15 major metals (copper, lead, tin, zinc, iron ore, manganese, nickel, chromium, cobalt, molybdenum, tungsten, vanadium, bauxite, titanium, and lithium), after Russia, South Africa, and the US (WRI 1992, pp. 262–3). However, if population size is taken into account, China's natural resources are not richer than in the world as a whole. For instance, with the exceptions of tin and tungsten, China's per capita

Table 3.1 Shares in Consumption of Primary Commodities for China, India, and the US (%)

Commodity		China	India	US
Metals 2005	Aluminum	22.5 (1)	3.0 (8)	19.4 (2)
	Copper	21.6 (1)	2.3 (11)	13.8 (2)
	Lead	25.7 (1)	1.3 (15)	19.4 (2)
	Nickel	15.2 (1)	0.9 (17)	9.5 (3)
	Tin	33.3 (1)	2.2 (7)	12.1 (2)
	Zinc	28.6 (1)	3.1 (8)	9.0 (2)
	Iron ore	29.0 (1)	4.8 (5)	4.7 (6)
	Steel production	31.5 (1)	3.5 (7)	8.5 (3)
Energy 2003	Coal	32.9 (1)	7.1 (3)	20.6 (2)
	Oil	7.4 (2)	3.4 (7)	25.3 (1)
	Total primary energy	12.6 (2)	3.6 (5)	23.4 (1)
	Electricity generation	11.4 (2)	3.8 (5)	24.3 (1)

Note: Figures within parentheses are world rankings.
Source: Streifel, S. "Impact of China and India on Global Commodity Markets: Focus on Metals and Minerals and Petroleum." Draft, Development Prospects Group, Washington D.C.: World Bank, 2006.

metal reserves are fewer than the world's, as shown in Table 3.2. In addition, China's metal resources are generally known to be low grade. For example, most of the iron ore reserves are found to be ferriferously poor, and the iron-rich ore that can be directly processed by refineries accounts for a little portion of the proven reserves; China's copper ore reserves can only be refined at a much lower rate of copper products than in many other countries. The phosphoric ore also has very little composition of phosphorus pentoxide (P_2O_5).

With the exception of hydropower resources, which are concentrated in the Southwest and Central South regions, energy resources are richer in the north than in the south; while metals are distributed principally in the geologically transitional area (such as Sichuan, Gansu, Hunan, and so on) between the plateau in the west and the mountain

Table 3.2 Major Metal Reserves of China and the World

ITEM	Million Tons of Contents			Per Capita Kg		
	China (1)	World (2)	(1)/(2) (%)	China (3)	World (4)	(3)/(4) (%)
Bauxite	150	21 559	0.70	128.2	3934.1	3.26
Copper	3.00	321.00	0.93	2.56	58.58	4.37
Iron ore	3 500	64 648	5.41	2992	11797	25.36
Lead	6.00	70.44	8.52	5.13	12.85	39.92
Manganese	13.6	812.8	1.67	11.62	148.32	7.83
Molybdenum	0.55	6.10	9.02	0.47	1.11	42.34
Nickel	0.73	48.66	1.50	0.62	8.88	6.98
Tin	1.50	5.93	25.30	1.28	1.08	118.52
Titanium	30.0	288.6	10.40	25.64	52.66	48.68
Tungsten	1.05	2.35	44.68	0.90	0.43	209.30
Vanadium	0.61	4.27	14.29	0.52	0.78	66.67
Zinc	5.00	143.90	3.47	4.27	36.26	16.26

Source: World Resources Institute (WRI). *World Resources 1992–93*. Oxford: Oxford University Press, 1992, pp. 322–3.

and hilly areas in the east. The regional distribution of China's major mineral resources is as follows:[2]

- Argentum (Ag): Jiangxi, Guangdong, Guangxi, Yunnan, Hunnan
- Bauxite: Shanxi, Henan, Shandong, Guangxi, Guizhou
- Bismuth (Bi): Hunan, Guangdong, Jiangxi, Yunnan, Inner Mongolia
- Chromium (Cr): Tibet, Inner Mongolia, Gansu
- Coal: Shanxi, Inner Mongolia, Shaanxi, Guizhou, Ningxia
- Collat. (Co): Gansu, Yunnan, Shandong, Hebei, Shanxi
- Copper (Cu): Jiangxi, Tibet, Yunnan, Gansu, Anhui
- Gold (Au): Shandong, Jiangxi, Heilongjiang, Jilin, Hubei
- Hydragyrum (Hg): Guizhou, Shaanxi, Hunan, Sichuan, Yunnan

- Iron (Fe) ore: Liaoning, Sichuan, Hebei, Shanxi, Anhui
- Kaolin (Ka): Hunan, Jiangsu, Fujian, Guangdong, Liaoning
- Lead (Pb): Yunnan, Guangdong, Hunan, Inner Mongolia, Jiangxi
- Manganese (Mn): Guangxi, Hunan, Guizhou, Liaoning, Sichuan
- Molybdenum (Mo): Henan, Jilin, Shaanxi, Shandong, Jiangxi
- Natural gas: Sichuan, Liaoning, Henan, Xinjiang, Hebei, Tianjin
- Nickel (Ni): Gansu, Yunnan, Jilin, Sichuan, Hubei
- Petroleum: Heilongjiang, Shandong, Liaoning, Hebei, Xinjiang
- Platinum (Pt): Gansu, Yunnan, Sichuan
- Silica stone (SiO_2): Qinghai, Beijing, Liaoning, Gansu, Sichuan
- Stibium (Sb): Hunan, Guangxi, Guizhou, Yunnan
- Tantalum (Ta): Jiangxi, Inner Mongolia, Guangdong, Hunan, Sichuan
- Tin (Sn): Guangxi, Yunnan, Hunan, Guangdong, Jiangxi
- Titanium (Ti): Sichuan, Hebei, Shaanxi, Shanxi
- Tungsten (WO_3): Hunan, Jiangxi, Henan, Fujian, Guangxi
- Vanadium (V): Sichuan, Hunan, Gansu, Hubei, Anhui
- Zinc (Zn): Yunnan, Inner Mongolia, Guangdong, Hunan, Gansu.

Figure 3.1 shows that the three resource-rich provinces (Sichuan, Shanxi, and Inner Mongolia) have almost a half of the nation's minerals. However, the 12 provinces (Guangdong, Hainan, Jilin, Guangxi, Jiangsu, Hubei, Beijing, Tianjin, Fujian, Zhejiang, Tibet, and Shanghai) as a whole account for only 5 percent of the total reserves. Energy resources are also unevenly distributed in China. Specifically, most of the hydropower reserves are concentrated in the Southwest and Central South regions; most coal reserves are distributed in the North and Northeast regions, with only a small portion, sparsely distributed, in the Northeast, East, and Central South regions. The Northeast and Northwest regions account for more than half of the nation's petroleum and natural gas reserves. In addition, the

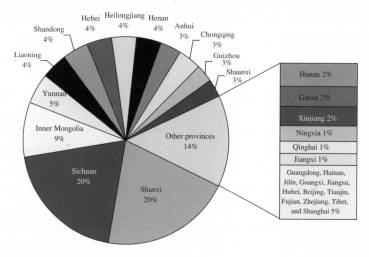

Notes
1 "Other provinces" include Guangdong, Hainan, Jilin, Guangxi, Jiangsu, Hubei, Beijing, Tianjin, Fujian, Zhejiang, Tibet, and Shanghai.
2 Sichuan and Chongqing are estimated by the author based on their total reserves and land areas proportionally.
Source: Created by the author, based on Sun, J. *Territory, Resources, and Regional Development* (in Chinese). Beijing: People's Education Press, 1987, pp. 4–8, for the monetary values of 45 major minerals.

Figure 3.1   Spatial distribution of major mineral resources in China

Northwest is the only region that is modestly rich in coal, hydropower, petroleum, and natural gas.

Coal resources are concentrated in the North and Northwest regions, around 600–1,000 km away from the most industrialized provinces and municipalities in the Southeast. Coal is transported mainly by train, and it accounts for more than 40 percent of the country's rail freight. On the other hand, the building of thermal power stations near the coalmines (*kengkou dianzhan*) seems to be an efficient solution, but faces substantial obstacles because of the shortage of water needed for turbine cooling. With an annual production of near 2.5 billion tons in 2008, coal accounts for more than 70 percent of China's primary energy production. This figure already makes China the world's leading coal producer. Furthermore, the Chinese coal industry is planning to increase its levels of annual coal production and it is unclear whether or not the Chinese government will be willing to introduce significant decreases in the current proportion of coal in total energy consumption in the foreseeable future. Environmental problems associated with the entire process of coal extraction, transportation, processing, and consumption will, therefore, continue to have a serious effect on the sustainable development in China if no measures are adopted.

China's dependence on coal continues amid the frequent occurrence of coalmine accidents, which cause thousands of casualties each year. Furthermore, China is much more inefficient in its coal exploitation than developed nations. At present, China uses about 3.3 tons of coal reserves in order to produce one ton of raw coal. In the US, for example, the production of one ton of raw coal uses only 1.25 tons of reserves. According to a report released by the Chinese Academy of Social Sciences, the mining recovery ratio has been less than 44 percent in China's large state-owned coal mines and only 10 percent in the small and private coal mines; by contrast, those in developed nations including Australia, Canada, Germany, and the US reportedly achieve figures as high as 80 percent (Cui 2007). The Chinese government has planned to raise the average recovery ratio of coal exploitation from the current figure of 30 percent to at least 50 percent by 2010 (Si 2008). As part of its efforts to achieve these goals, China has decided to consolidate the coal industry by building several large mining conglomerates (each with a production capacity of 100 million tons of raw coal per year), as well as to shut down those small and inefficient coal pits. However, this seems to be a difficult job to realize in a short period, since many stakeholders, especially local governments, are unwilling to support this kind of reform.

Currently, petroleum and natural gas are supplied mainly by the Northeast and Northwest regions. Oil and gas reserves are rich in China's continental shelves. However, China has maritime disputes with Japan in the East China Sea, with North Korea and, possibly, South Korea in the

Yellow Sea, and with other Southeast nations in the South China Sea. In addition, the locational disadvantages of offshore oil/gas fields in these sea areas will pose difficulties for China's seabed oil/gas exploitation and transportation. Theoretically, the structure of energy consumption may be largely readjusted through foreign trade. As a result of its rapidly growing consumption—and relatively stagnant production—of petroleum, in 1993 China became a net importer of oil. According to the Economist Intelligence Agency (EIA), China's consumption of petroleum increased by 3.44 times to 13.11 quadrillion BTU in 2004 from 3.81 quadrillion BTU in 1980, while its production of crude oil increased only 1.65 times to 7.50 quadrillion BTU in 2004 from 4.55 quadrillion BTU in 1980, creating an ever-growing oil shortage. In addition, China's oil deficit stood at 3.5 million barrels per day in 2006 and is expected to quadruple to 13.1 million barrels per day over the projection period to 2030, when the country's oil consumption is projected to reach 15.7 million barrels per day (EIA 2006). That is to say, more than 80 percent of China's oil demand should be met by either imports or technological substitution.

The government hopes to reduce the share of thermal power in its power generation mix through the construction of large hydroelectric dams. The main hydroelectric dams are Gezhouba Dam in Hubei province, followed by Liujiaxia Dam in Gansu province, Longyang Dam in Qinghai province, Manwan Dam in Yunnan province, Baishan Dam in Jilin province, and so on. China has now also completed the world's largest dam in the Three Gorges on the Yangtze River. This dam increases the supply of affordable electricity throughout the Yangtze Valley, as well as controlling floods, boosting the growing economy, and reducing the levels of air pollution. The economic advantages coming from such a big dam, however, could also be reduced by the losses arising from the ecological and environmental costs and risks.

The Chinese leadership realizes that the development of nuclear power is an appropriate solution to improve local energy shortages in those eastern and southern coastal areas that lack coal and petroleum resources. Currently, the nuclear power stations are at Qinshan in

Zhejiang province, Daya Bay in Guangdong province, and Hongyanhe in Liaoning province.

With its large land mass and long coastline, China has relatively abundant wind resources. The windiest areas of the country are located mainly along the southeast coast and the nearby islands; in Inner Mongolia, Xinjiang, and western Gansu; and in some parts of Northeast China, Northwest China, North China, and the Qinghai-Tibetan Plateau. Apart from this, there are also certain areas in China's interior that are rich in wind resources. China has large marine areas, and ocean-based wind resources are plentiful.

ENVIRONMENTAL QUALITY

China's environmental concerns stem from two kinds of human activities: (1) resource depletion, which covers the losses reflecting the deterioration of land and depleting reserves of coal, petroleum, timber, groundwater, and so on; and (2) resource degradation, which covers the consequences associated with air and water pollution, land erosion, solid wastes, and so on. Resource depletion is a concern because it would mean the quantitative exhaustion of natural resources that are an important source of revenues, obtained through exploitation and the discovery of new reserves. In the case of resource degradation, the issue is not the quantitative exhaustion of natural resources, but rather the qualitative degradation of the ecosystem; for example, through, among other things, the contamination of air and water as a result of the generation and deposit of residuals, and as a result of the environmental impact of producing garbage and solid wastes.

In order to make an assessment of China's environmental situation, let us consider air, water, land, and deforestation and desertification.

Air

Recent decades have seen a worsening of China's air quality, particularly in urban areas. According to European satellite data, pollutants in the sky over China have increased by about 50 percent between 1995 and 2005.

The satellite data also revealed that the city of Beijing—China's capital—is one of the worst environmental victims of China's spectacular economic growth, which has led to air pollution levels that have been blamed for more than 400,000 premature deaths a year. According to the European Space Agency, Beijing and its neighboring northeast provinces have the planet's worst levels of nitrogen dioxide, which can cause fatal damage to the lungs (Watts 2005). An explosive increase in car owner-ship is blamed for a sharp rise in unhealthy emissions.

In 2006 China became the largest national producer of greenhouse gas (GHG) emissions, with an estimated annual production of about 6,200 million tons, which is followed by the US, with about 5,800 million tons (see Table 3.3). When discussing the situation of China's GHG emissions, one comes across two different opinions: first, it is posited that the country's per capita emissions are very low in comparison with the industrially developed countries and that the *onus* of global warming must rest elsewhere; second, compared with other countries, China's GHG emissions per unit of GDP are already very high—approximately 5.36 times that of the US—in 2006, although this figure has been reduced compared to that in 1990. According to its long-term commitment, which was announced at the United Nations Climate Change Conference, held in Copenhagen from December 7 to 18, 2009, China has also agreed to cut the intensity of carbon dioxide emissions per unit of GDP in 2020 by 40 to 45 percent from 2005 levels.

In China, atmospheric pollution comes mainly from the burning of coal and its associated products that, under the most optimistic scenario, will be unlikely to contribute less than the current three-quarters of total primary energy consumption by the year 2025 or even by the year 2050. China's chlorofluorocarbon (CFC) and halon com-pound use is relatively minor given the size of the country. However, the potential for much greater use of CFCs is enormous. Moreover, it is projected that CFC emissions are projected to increase as a result of both China's economic growth and its increases in population. The specific sources of these emissions are, in order of quantity produced, livestock, wet rice, natural gas pipeline leakage, solid waste disposal,

Table 3.3 Greenhouse Gas (GHG) Emissions, China and the US

Item	China		US	
	1990	2006	1990	2006
GDP (billion US$)[a]	372.4	2,626.3	5,672.6	13,194.7
GHGs (million ton)	2,524	6,200	5,163	5,800
GHGs/POP (ton/person)	2.18	4.72	21.0	19.4
GHGs/LA (ton/km^2)	262.9	645.8	551.6	619.7
GHGs/GDP (kg/US$)	6.78	2.36	0.91	0.44

[a] Measured in exchange rates (for China) and in current prices (for China and the US).
Notes: GDP = gross national product, POP = population, LA = land area.
Source: Calculated by the author based on WRI World Resources 1992–93. Oxford: Oxford University Press, 1992, and NEAA, 'China Now No. 1 in CO_2 Emissions; USA in Second Position'. Netherlands Environmental Assessment Agency (NEAA), 2007. Available at www.mnp.nl.

and coal mining. In addition, China's large and still expanding population also suggests a concomitant increase of methane (CH_4).

Most of China's proven coal reserves are bituminous, with only a small proportion being lignite and anthracite. Therefore, coal is mainly responsible not only for the high carbon dioxide (CO_2) emissions, but also for the high emissions of sulfur (SO_2), nitrogen oxide (NO_x), and total suspended particulate (TSP). In addition, as the northern (especially urban) areas usually use coal for heating in the winter, it is unsurprising that the level of air pollution there is much more serious than that in the southern part. All of these pollutants pose serious threats to public health. There has been a rise in the share of chronic obstructive pulmonary disease and cancers. In addition, acid rain is becoming an increasingly critical issue. The high sulfur content of burning coal contributes widely to the high acidity levels of rainfall. Nationwide acid rain measurement shows that the situation is particularly serious in southern China, where the pH values are often lower than 5.6—a value indicative of acid rain.

Another noticeable factor is that the wind coming from the Northwest region increases the neutralizing capability of atmosphere and transfers air pollutants to Southeast China and the neighboring countries.

Water

The constant and excessive extraction of groundwater has led to the continuous dropping of the water table and the subsidence of land. The area of subsidence around large municipalities such as Beijing, Tianjin, and Shanghai has been reported to be the most serious. In the coastal areas of Hebei and Shandong provinces, the excessive drop in the groundwater level has led to the leeching of saline water into the freshwater aquifers. In the loess plateau area of Northwest China, the drawing of underground water for irrigation is becoming extremely difficult, with increasing energy costs. Another key issue is the pollution of drinking water in both urban and rural areas. Many groundwater sources have been affected as a result of infiltration of polluted surface water in urban areas. Rural water resources are even more contaminated due to fertilizers and pesticide runoff, human and animal waste, and pollutants from the township and village-owned enterprises. As a result, many people residing in the rural areas have no access to safe drinking water.

River water pollution in those sections of rivers that run through or near cities is the most serious in terms of ammonia nitrogen, fecal bacteria, volatile phenols, and biological oxygen demands (BOD).[3] The Huaihe River, which many people now refer to as the *black river*, has been the most polluted river in China. The Yangtze River, which closely connects China's large industrial bases such as Chongqing, Wuhan, Nanjing, and Shanghai, will become, as believed by many observers, more seriously polluted, if no countermeasure is carried out. In addition, pollution from heavy metals, such as mercury (Hg), lead (Pb), and other toxic chemicals are also having a serious impact on river water.

Nitrogen and phosphorus pollution is common in China's lakes. Water pollution has not only endangered the local fishery and the collection of limnological plants, but has also affected the daily lives and health of the nearby residents. In addition, petropollutants, inorganic nitrogen, and inorganic phosphorus are common in the coastal water sources. Marine environments near large coastal cities are degraded as a result of the discharge of raw sewage and coastal construction. As a result, incidences of red tides have become frequent in many coastal areas, contaminated fish and mollusks have been commonplace, and consequently many fragile marine environments have been destroyed. Marine pollution in northeastern and southern China is of particular concern since the industrial development is outpacing the environmental protection efforts in these areas.

The excessive use of water without adequate drainage leads to water logging, salinization, and soil erosion. Salinization and alkalization are increasingly affecting irrigated farmland. In the Northeast region, cropping activities have increased the soil alkalinity to such a high level that it is very difficult to put them back into pasture. In the sandy soils of the Northwest region, where the irrigation water seeps away quickly, strong winds and high evaporation contribute to easy alkalization of the soil. The rapid development of individually and collectively owned industrial enterprises are generally known to be responsible for the increasing levels of water pollution in rural areas. More than two-thirds of China's industrial wastewater has flown directly into rivers, lakes, seas, and reservoirs. The chemical industry is the largest wastewater producer. Other main sectors discharging wastewater include ferrous metals, papermaking and paper products, the production and supply of power, steam and hot water, and so on.

Land

Since the introduction of economic reforms in the late 1970s, the transference of farmland to residential and industrial uses has been promoted. Consequently, the area of land under cultivation has decreased substantially. This meant that in order to increase the level of agricultural production, the only way was to increase the levels of land productivity, which resulted in the intensive use of chemical fertilizers, continuous cropping, greatly expanded irrigation, and the use of improved plant varieties. In practice, it is almost impossible for farmers to make an accurate count of the proportion of nutrients that is required by the soil. In most cases, the marginal cost and benefit do not encourage the use of fertilizers. The government's subsidies on fertilizer consumption could distort the pricing mechanism and induce farmers to the even more excessive and inefficient use of chemical fertilizers, which has, through the leaching of nitrates, caused the contamination of groundwater and the deterioration of soil structure.

Organic manure and the leavened crop residues, stalks, and straws have many advantages when used as fertilizers, even if their value of nutrient per unit volume is lower than that of chemical fertilizers. Many farmers, however, have ignored the advantages of these *clean* fertilizers. In addition, in rural China the shortage of fuel wood for both cooking and heating results in the burning of straws, stalks, and crop residues. Continuous cropping, instead of crop rotation, may cause the soil to be deficient in some nutrients. For example, the cropping of soybeans causes a deficiency of phosphorus and potassium in the soil. The use of high-yielding and improved plant varieties has made crops more vulnerable to pest damage, which results in the use of pesticides. Since the 1970s the use of pesticides has increased in both tonnage and concentration of active ingredients and, as a result, has had a serious effect on water, soil, and food.

The more widespread use of plastic sheeting is a further threat. Farmers have been increasingly interested in the application of plastic sheets to conserve soil moisture and speed up the maturation of crops, particularly in northern China. But many farmers have ignored the fact that plastic sheets, if not treated properly after cropping, may be mixed with the soil and hence hinder the flow of water and root growth. Farmland is also suffering from the damages of industrial wastes and urban rubbish, occupied by piles of solid waste and seriously damaged as a result of the improper use of garbage and sludge. The sum of these circumstances has led to soil loss, especially in the area where ground cover was removed. The ecosystems of forests, wetlands, sloping, and marginal lands are particularly fragile. Another form of soil contamination is the use of wastewater for irrigation, which ignores the fact that acids and toxic heavy metals in much of this water impair the soil chemistry and render it useless for agriculture.

Apart from the soil loss deriving from the erosion process, another consequence of soil over-exploitation and removal of ground cover is the increase of silt materials flowing into rivers. This leads to the rising of riverbeds undermining flood control, navigation, and power-generating capacity. The loess plateau area between Gansu, Shaanxi, and Shanxi provinces has been cultivated since the Neolithic period and is now perhaps one of the most erosion-prone areas in the world. Through this area, the Yellow River carries billions of tons of sediment annually into the Bohai Sea by degrading the land seriously. The average riverbed has been rising by approximately one meter per decade with a consequent growing risk of catastrophic flooding. The Yangtze River's load raises lake levels, particularly in Hubei and Hunan provinces. As a result, over the course of recent decades most lakes in East Hubei have disappeared, owing to the combination of silting and conversion to farmland.

With the formation of cones of depression, many cities, especially those coastal cities that have thick unconsolidated soft soil layers, are suffering from land subsidence caused by the withdrawal of underground water in deep aquifers. The cities of Shanghai and Tianjin, with a maximum subsidence of about three meters, are the most severe cases. Ground subsidence has caused a series of problems, such as the sinking and splitting of railway bases, buildings, and underground pipelines, and an emerging flooding crisis in areas near major rivers or the sea. For example, embankments have had to be constructed to prevent flooding of seawater into some areas of Tianjin after significant ground subsidence.

Deforestation and Desertification

The causes of deforestation come mainly from the rapidly growing population in rural areas and the economic interests of the state. As the size of population expands, the needs of food, housing, and energy will increase accordingly. The conversion of forestland, grassland, and wetland to cropland, as well as the illegal felling of trees for lumber and fuel, increases. In the rural areas, the lack of fuels led to use of wood for both heating and cooking. But the traditional rural stoves have low combustion efficiency. In addition, much of the fuel wood consumed is low-quality brush and weeds collected from already deforested hills.

From the 1950s to the 1970s, a period during which a series of political and social movements (such as the Great Leap Forward and the Cultural Revolution) were under way, many of China's natural and tropical forests were suffering serious damage. In Tibet and many other provinces and autonomous regions, the process of forest degradation began with the large-scale cutting of forests by the state or its contractors for commercial logging. This large-scale cutting combined with fuel necessities has denuded hillsides, resulting in soil erosion and water loss. Covering about one-third of its total land area, China's grassland is concentrated in the Inner Mongolia, Xinjiang, and Tibet autonomous regions, and a few other provinces and autonomous regions, located mostly in the North and Northwest regions. As grassland is regarded as "wasteland" in some rural areas, the conversion of it into productive uses has been promoted as a result of the growth in population. The conversion of grassland into crop cultivation has led to a continuing decrease in the amount of grassland.

Heavy and frequent sand storms in northern China have resulted in damage to the sustainability of the Chinese economy. Dust storms are caused by turbulent wind systems that contain particles of dust that reduce visibility to less than 1,000 m. A dust storm may cause soil erosion, loess formation, climate change, air pollution, and a reduction in the level of solar irradiance. Although the number of annual dust days has decreased over past decades, the frequency of severe dust storms (where visibility is less than 200 m) has increased during the same period in northern China, with four in the 1950s, seven in the 1960s, 13 in the 1970s, 14 in the 1980s, and 23 in the 1990s (Qian and Zhu 2001; and Chen et al. 2003). An extremely dry environment can induce more severe dust storms such as the "Black Storm" (in which visibility was less than 10 m).

The variability of dust storms over time is associated with climate fluctuations in terms of both temperature and precipitation. The arid and semi-arid areas of northern China make up 30 percent of the country's total land area; and the dry mid-latitude climate is dominated by continental polar air masses much of the year. Most dust events occur during the spring season from March to May when cyclonic cold fronts meets warm air mass influxes, leading to strong seasonal atmospheric instability, a favorable synoptic condition for dust storms. However, human activities have also had a substantial impact on dust storms at both regional and local levels. In northern China, there was a rapid escalation of the level of desertified land, as a direct result of human activity. In recent decades the Chinese government has invested substantial social and economic resources to suppress dust storms. Despite some successful cases, the present-day desertification situation is not optimistic.

In China, environmental concerns have stemmed from two kinds of human activities: resource depletion, which covers the losses reflecting the deterioration of land and depleting reserves of coal, petroleum, timber, groundwater, and so on; resource degradation, which is associated with air and water pollution, land erosion, solid wastes, and so on. Resource depletion is a concern because it leads to the quantitative exhaustion of natural resources that are an important source of revenues, obtained through exploitation and the discovery of new reserves. In the case of resource degradation, the issue is not the quantitative exhaustion of natural resources, but rather the qualitative degradation of the ecosystem—for example, through the contamination of air and water as a result of the generation and deposit of residuals, and as a result of the environmental impact of producing garbage and solid waste.

POLICY IMPLICATIONS

The vast size and diversified natural conditions in China have generated many regional differences in terms of climate, geography, soil fertility, and other resource endowments, which in turn mean that the living standards vary from region to region. In particular, the South and East regions have natural advantages for agriculture over the Northwest region. Minerals and energy resources are much richer in the North than in the South. In other aspects, the eastern coastal area, because of its geographical proximity to market economies, may find it easier to introduce the *laissez-faire* approach than would be the case for the central and the western inland areas. All of these factors have inevitably resulted in great economic disparities among regions.

The uneven distribution of natural resources in China has had a considerable influence on the "disequilibrated" regional structures of exploitation and the supply of those resources used as inputs of production to produce desired final goods and services for the society. China's mineral and energy resources are principally distributed in the northern and western inland areas, while the largest industrial consumers are located in the eastern and southern coastal areas. There-fore, the long-distance transfers of raw materials and semi-finished products from the northern and western inland areas to the eastern and southern coastal areas should be the only feasible approach by which to efficiently create an equilibrium between supply and demand in the Chinese economy. The Chinese government should recognize this fact and try to deal carefully with national economic cooperation.

In contrast to the development pattern of most industrialized economies, the Chinese economy has been fueled principally by coal rather than by petroleum and natural gas. Given its abundance in reserves compared with other energy resources such as hydropower, petroleum and natural gas, coal, which accounts for more than 80 percent of China's total energy resources, has until recently supplied almost 70 percent of the nation's total energy supply. Without stressing the low heating conversion rate of coal consumption, the serious environmental damage resulting from the exploitation, transportation, and consumption of coal resources has already posed challenges to the sustainable development of the Chinese economy.

During recent decades, China's rapid economic development has resulted in a substantial improvement in the standard of living of ordinary people. However, it has also generated environmental problems at an alarmingly high rate. Carbon dioxide (CO_2), sulfur (SO_2), nitrogen oxide (NO_x), methane (CH_4), chlorofluorocarbons (CFCs), and other hazardous waste and toxic materials have been increasingly produced in parallel with industrial growth in China. Air pollution stemming from the burning of coal—China's major primary energy—has reached the approximate level of the developed countries in the 1950s and 1960s. Today, air, water, noise pollution, and land erosion, together with unprocessed garbage, have had a considerable impact on Chinese society. One striking example is that air pollution is estimated to have caused more than 400,000 excess deaths in 2003, and this figure will increase if no action is taken (Winters and Yusuf 2007, p. 26).

Since the late 1970s, several changes have taken place in the legislation of environmental protection in China, along with the economic reform and opening up to the outside world. The year 1978 saw the first insertion of a clause for environmental protection in the Constitution of the People's Republic of China. China's first Law on Environmental Protection (*huanjing baohu fa*) was formally promulgated in 1989 and was further revised in 1995. Since the early 1980s, a series of laws, regulations, and national standards (*guobiao*, or GB) concerning environmental protection have been promulgated in China. A relatively comprehensive legal system concerning environmental protection has initially taken shape. China has joined or approved many international protocols on environmental protection, including the United Nations Convention on the Law of the Sea (UNCLOS), the Antarctic Treaty, the Convention on International Trade in Endangered Species, the Vienna Conference for the Protection of the Ozone Layer, the Basel Convention on Transboundary Hazardous Waste Disposal, the Montreal Protocol for Limiting use of CFCs, the Kyoto Protocol, and so on. However, Chinese legislation faces problems of attempting to achieve coordination and consistency with international treaties and conventions.

China has essentially followed a traditional development model that is characterized by high resource and energy (mainly coal) consumption and extensive management. This has led not only to environmental damage, but it has also affected its economic sustainability. Therefore, shifting the development strategy and embarking on the path to sustainable development is the only correct choice for the Chinese economy. In this chapter we have posed questions about China's natural resources and environmental issues rather than drawing any conclusions. It should be noted that China, like many other developing countries, is facing many pressing problems related to the economic development that might, at least in the short run, be contradicted by a system of environmental protection. However, environmental policies and measures should never be treated independently from economic policies. More importantly, they can serve as a dynamic mechanism for the maximization of the real wellbeing of the whole people.

ENDNOTES

1 The exception that proves the rule is aluminum, for which China is a net exporter and produces about 25% of the world total. Compared with price increases of 379% for copper from January 2002 to June 2006, aluminum prices have increased modestly—up only 80% (Streifel 2006).
2 Judged by the author based on CISNR (1990, p. 644). Note that only major resource-rich provinces are listed in order of reserves and that Guangdong and Sichuan include Hainan province and Chongqing municipality, respectively.
3 As oxygen is required to aerobically decompose biologically degradable compounds, the higher the level of BOD, the poorer the water quality.

CHAPTER FOUR

THE FOUNDATION OF THE CHINESE ECONOMY (II)

The Qin Terra-cotta Warriors, Xi'an

A huge population does not represent an advantage in human resources for economic development. This is particularly true for China, which is being transformed from an agricultural society that has used mainly traditional methods of production to an industrial society that requires not only advanced sciences and technologies, but also qualified workers. A well-educated and law-abiding population that possesses a strong work ethic is the *sine qua non* of China's economic growth. In addition, Chinese culture, which aims to achieve a harmonious balance between Confucianism, Buddhism, and Taoism, worked particularly well over a very long period of time. However, the early cultural achievements sometimes may become an obstacle to innovation . . .

> Mt. Tai did not refuse every block of soil, so it has become a great mountain; the Yellow River and the East Sea did not refuse small streams, so they achieve their depth; and the Kings did not refuse a large number of people, so they enjoyed respect of merit. Therefore, land should not be divided into the East and the West; and no people should be treated as foreigners . . . Now Your Majesty intends to abandon the people to subsidize the enemy and expel the guest scholars who might contribute to the other states' achievements. Consequently, the Magi around the world would stop their footsteps at the entrance into the state of Qin. Ah! This is what people said, "lending weapons to enemies, and giving dry rations to thieves."
>
> —*Li Si (c.* 280–208 BC)

POPULATION

At the beginning of the twenty-first century, China's population is above 1.3 billion, which accounts for more than 20 percent of the global total; it is nine times that of Japan, about five times that of the US, and three times that of the entire European Union. Moreover, China's population has continued to grow at a rate of more than 10 million per annum. In the coming decades, China will continue to be the world's most populous nation before the mid-twenty-first century, when, according to the projection by the United Nations Population Division (UNPD), it will be overtaken by India (UNPD 2007).

The dynamic mechanism of population growth has been substantially influenced by China's population policies. When the PRC was founded in 1949, the population of mainland China was about 450 million. Since then China has experienced two major peaks of population growth. From 1949 to 1958, when the Great Leap Forward movement was launched, the birth rate was as high as 3 to 4 percent, while, in contrast, the death rate decreased significantly. This dramatic growth in population was largely encouraged by the government in line with Mao Zedong's thought "the greater the population, the easier it is for things to be done." China's population began to grow rapidly once again after the famine period (1959–61), during which millions of people died from starvation. The birth rate peaked at 4.3 percent in 1963 and then decreased gradually, but still ran at over 2 percent until the early 1970s when the government realized the importance of population control (see Figure 4.1).

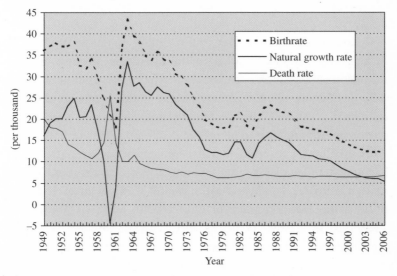

Figure 4.1   Birth, death, and natural growth rates

The Chinese government's promotion of its "sea of manpower" approach led simultaneously to the development of a number of population problems. During recent decades, when the population densities of some developed countries has either stayed constant or decreased gradually, China's population density has increased sharply from 40 persons per square kilometer of land area in 1949 up to 130 persons per square kilometer of land area at the end of the 1990s—a figure that is more than three times that of the world as a whole. In fact, China's population density is not very high when compared with South Korea (443 persons per km^2), Japan (329 persons per km^2), India (290 persons per km^2), the UK (237 persons per km^2), and Germany (226 persons per km^2). However, because much of China's territory consists of mountains, desert, and other uninhabitable lands, the number of persons per square kilometer of the *inhabitable* land area is much larger than the nominal population density in China. For instance, the population densities of many provinces in East China are more than 400 persons per square kilometer of land area (see Figure 4.2), much higher than that of most of the most populous nations in the world.

Mao Zedong, faced by the grim reality of population growth, in his later years even acknowledged the increasing pressure of over-population on the Chinese economy, when he began to puzzle about his earlier prediction that "Of all things in the world, people are the most precious. . . . Even if China's population multiplies many times, she is fully capable of finding a solution" (Mao 1949, pp. 453–4). In the early 1970s, the Chinese government had to implement a birth control policy that aimed to encourage late marriages, prolong the time period between births and reduce the number of children in each family. In 1978, the encouragement of birth control made its first official appearance in Article 53 of the PRC Constitution. Following the implementation of a population control policy, the First National Conference on Birth Control was held in Beijing in 1979. The conference requested "that one couple has only one child and at most two children, but with a three-year interval. Those couples who do not plan to have a second child will be rewarded and those who have a third child will receive economic punishment."

Since the 1970s, and especially since the early 1980s, China has effectively controlled its population trends with the introduction of a series of strict measures. The rate of population growth rate declined dramatically—from 3 percent in the 1960s to less than 1 percent by the end of the 1990s. Obviously, without this reduction, China's population would have increased by more than 20 million (that is, $(0.03 - 0.01) \times 1$ billion) per annum. In other words, as a result of China's population control efforts, every two or three years the increase in population has been reduced by an amount equal to the size a medium-sized nation such as the UK or France. Furthermore, the reduction of population growth also increased China's per capita GNP by more than 2 percent.[1] Despite these successes, some problems still remain.

First, China's population control policy has generated a gender imbalance. In the poorest and most remote rural areas, the traditional discrimination against women remains very strong. Because there is very little social security in those rural areas, sons offer the best hope for parents who are still earning their living by physical labor. This provides a strong incentive for people to have more than one child until they have son(s). Partly as a result of the birth control policy and partly because of the increasing burden of having an additional child (girl), the inhumane practice of foeticide and infanticide can be occasionally found, especially in rural areas where men generally have a higher social position than women. China's national birth gender proportion (that is, male to female) is much higher than that found in the developed nations. If only the rural area is taken into account, the birth gender difference would be even larger.

Second, a lower birth rate will result eventually in a higher proportion of aged people. This is already a social problem in the advanced nations and, sooner or later, it will also affect the Chinese society. Thanks to the government's efforts in raising the social position of women and the strict domicile system for urban citizens, China's "one-child" policy has been successfully implemented in the urban areas since the early 1980s. At present, it is very common in urban China for a couple to have only one child. However, the policy is to rigidly transform China's urban family pattern into a reverse pyramid in the coming decades. In China in 1953, the ratio of the population aged 65 or over was only 4.4 percent percent. This ratio was further reduced to 3.6 percent in 1964, but rose again to 4.9 percent in 1982, 5.6 percent in 1990, and 7.0 percent in 2000.[2] The population age composition also differs from region to region. In 1982, Shanghai became the first province where the percentage of the population aged 65 years or over exceeded 7 percent of the total—a criterion that is generally thought to characterize an aging society. By the end of the 1990s, a number of other provinces could also share this classification: Beijing, Tianjin, Jiangsu, Zhejiang, Shandong, Guangdong, Liaoning, Sichuan, and so on.

Third, patterns of population growth show considerable differences between the rural and urban areas of China. In some poor rural areas, where labor productivity is to a large extent physically determined, parents have strong incentives to have large numbers of children. By contrast, in urban and other relatively well-off areas, parents who receive higher education and have lifetime social welfare usually have to make a trade-off between having more children and improving their living standards and quality of life. Faced with cramped living conditions and the high cost of education, as well as severe competition for university entrance, urban parents have little incentive to have a second child, not to mention the fact that those who illegally raise more than one child would not receive subsidies from the government and could be fired from their current posts. As an only child is, in general, better protected by its family than one with siblings, those children born in urban areas usually receive better care and education than those born in rural areas. In brief, the fact that the rural poor have more children than the urban and well-educated people will reduce the overall educational level of the Chinese population.

As a result of the diverse regional natural and geographical conditions, the population of China is unevenly distributed. Generally, population density is higher in the Eastern belt than in the Central belt, while the Central belt has a higher density than the Western belt. The most populous provinces are Shanghai (2,776 persons per km^2), Tianjin (909 persons per km^2), Beijing (821 persons per km^2), Jiangsu (736 persons per km^2), Shandong (603 persons per km^2), and Henan (598 persons per km^2). On the other hand, however, Tibet, Qinghai, Xinjiang, and Inner Mongolia have only 2, 7, 12, and 22 persons for each square kilometer of the land area, respectively (see Figure 4.2).

LABOR AND EDUCATION

As stated above, a huge population does not represent an advantage in human resources for economic development. This is particularly true for a country such as China, which is being transformed from an agricultural society that has used mainly traditional methods of production to an industrial society that requires not only advanced sciences and technologies, but also qualified workers. When labor supply exceeds labor demand, unemployment occurs. According to China's official definition, the registered unemployment rate in urban areas refers to the ratio of the number of the registered unemployed persons to the sum of the number of employed persons and the registered unemployed persons. The registered unemployed persons in urban areas are defined as: persons who are registered as permanent residents in the urban areas engaged in non-agricultural activities, aged within the range of working age (for male, 16 years or older, but younger than 50 years; for female, 16 years or older, but younger than 45 years), capable of work, and unemployed, but wishing to be employed and registered with the local employment service agencies.

A cross-national comparison of the economically active population—a term defined as "all men or women who simply work for the production of economic goods and services during a specific period" — shows that China had an incredibly high level of per capita annual labor input (947 hours), compared with the African nations (608 hours) and the Western nations (709 hours) (Maddison 1996, table J-1). The high

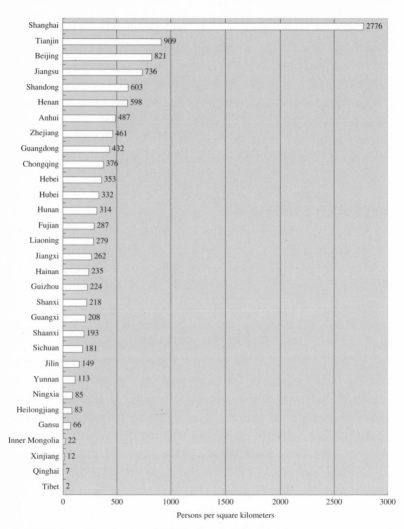

Figure 4.2   China's population density, by province

level of labor input may help us to understand, at least in part, China's rapid economic growth over the course of recent decades.

As mentioned at the beginning of this chapter, a well-educated and law-abiding population that possesses a strong work ethic is the *sine qua non* of China's economic growth. A human development index (HDI) has been computed by the United Nations Development Program (UNDP) for a number of countries. This is simply the average of indices for life expectancy, literacy and school enrollment, and price-adjusted PPP GDP per capita. Table 4.1 shows that: (1) internationally, China's

Table 4.1 China's Provincial Human Development Index (HDI), 2003

Nations	HDI	Chinese Provinces	HDI
Norway	0.96		
Hong Kong	0.92	Shanghai	0.91
South Korea	0.90	Beijing	0.88
Argentina	0.86	Tianjin	0.86
Mexico	0.81	Guangdong, Liaoning, Zhejiang, Jiangsu	0.81–0.82
Brazil, Malaysia, Colombia	0.79	Heilongjiang, Fujian	0.79
Thailand	0.78	Shandong, Hebei, Jilin	0.77–0.78
The Philippines	0.76	Hainan, Xinjiang, Hubei, Shanxi, Hunan, Chongqing	0.75–0.76
China in 2003	**0.75**		
Turkey	0.75	Henan, Inner Mongolia	0.74
China in 1999	**0.72**	Jiangxi, Guangxi, Shaanxi, Sichuan, Anhui	0.73
Indonesia, Vietnam	0.70	Ningxia	0.71
		Qinghai, Gansu	0.68
		Yunnan	0.66
China in 1990	**0.63**	Guizhou	0.64
India	0.60		
Myanmar	0.58	Tibet	0.59
China in 1980	**0.56**		
Pakistan	0.53		

Sources: UNDP and CDRF. *China Human Development Report 2005*. Beijing: UNDP and China Development Research Foundation (CDRF); and UNDP. *Human Development Report 2005: International Cooperation at a Crossroad*. New York: Oxford University Press, 2005, pp. 219–23. Cited from Naughton, B. *The Chinese Economy: Transitions and Growth*. Cambridge, MA: The MIT Press, 2007, p. 226.

HDI has improved significantly since 1980; and (2) domestically, there is significant variation among China's provinces. For example, we can see that Shanghai's HDI is comparable to Hong Kong's or South Korea's; and several coastal provinces have, like Mexico, inched into the high HDI category. However, several western provinces, such as Gansu, Yunnan, and Tibet are below Indonesia and Vietnam.

More than 2,500 years ago, Guan Zhong (725–645 BC)—a prime minister in the state of Qi during the Spring and Autumn period (771–475 BC) made a famous hypothesis on the economic return to education:

> If you plan for a year, sow a seed; for 10 years, plant a tree; for 100 years, teach the people. You will reap a single harvest by sowing a seed once and 10 harvests by planting a tree; while you will reap 100 harvests by teaching the people.

For more than 1,000 years, and as a result of Confucian influences, people in China have placed a substantial value on education. At present, most Chinese parents still believe it to be a glorious thing for their children to attain the highest school degrees. However, for the majority of the past 100 years, the development of education in China has not been particularly successful.

In 1964, when the second national population census was conducted, 56.76 percent of the total population aged 16 years of age and above were classified as either illiterate or semi-literate. Thereafter, the illiterate and semi-literate rate decreased considerably, but it was still estimated at 31.88 percent and 20.61 percent in the third and fourth national population census in 1982 and 1990, respectively. China's moderately high illiteracy has been determined by both historic and institutional factors. Before 1949, China's education was very backward and had been seriously damaged by the long-lasting wars. For instance, more than 60 percent of people born in the 1930s and more than 70 percent of people born in the 1920s were either illiterate or semi-literate. During the two peaks of population growth in the

1950s and the 1960s, neither the government nor their families were capable of providing an adequate educational opportunity for each child.

The period of the Cultural Revolution (1966–76) saw a substantial revision of China's education system that had, to a large extent, been grounded in the principles of Confucianism. The length of primary school education was reduced from six years to five years; and that of junior and senior middle schools was cut by one year in each instance. In addition, the textbooks were heavily revised and simplified. Even worse, the status of schoolteachers, who had been highly regarded in traditional Chinese society, became subject to political discrimination. At the same time, the destruction of the higher education system was even more severe because universities were closed during between 1966 and 1970, and operated in line with political rather than academic considerations between 1971 and 1976. The Cultural Revolution resulted in a "break-point" of ages for scientists and engineers, which has already had a negative effect on China's socioeconomic development.

China's educational system began to return to a more normal path as soon as the Cultural Revolution came to an end. In 1977 there was a resumption of the national entrance examinations for higher learning institutes. One year later, the Chinese government made the first recognition, during the First National Conference on Science and Technology, that "science and technology is a productive force," and began to treat intellectuals as "a branch of the working class." Since this declaration, education has been the subject of much state attention. In 1995, the Chinese government decided to implement a nine-year compulsory education system (that is, six years of primary school followed by three years of junior middle school), with the aim of achieving universal access to junior middle school within six years in urban and coastal areas and within 10 years in the other parts of the country.

In recent years, China's primary and junior middle education has achieved substantial progress, with the enrollment rates increased to nearly 100 percent in the early years of the twenty-first century. In the early 2000s, China's higher learning institutions (including three- and four-year colleges), which were only able to absorb a small proportion of graduates from senior middle schools before the 1990s and an even smaller proportion of them before the 1980s (data are not shown in Figure 4.3), have provided opportunities to more than two-thirds of senior middle school graduates. However, problems still remain in senior middle school education. For instance, almost one-third of graduates from junior middle schools have not been able to enter senior middle schools in the 2000s (see Figure 4.3).

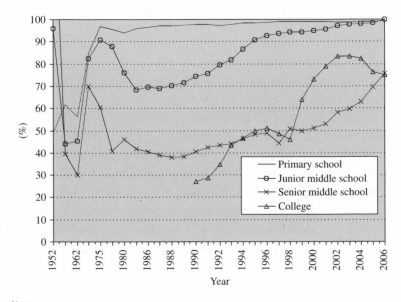

Notes
1 The proportion of graduates of junior middle schools entering senior middle schools was higher than 100 percent in the early 1950s, the students who graduated from junior middle schools were less than the students enrolled in senior middle schools.
2 Graduates of junior middle school include vocational schools.
3 "College," whose data are not available prior 1990, includes 3- and 4-year colleges.

Figure 4.3   Enrollment ratios of various educational institutions

TECHNOLOGICAL INNOVATION

Technological innovation has been the most fundamental element in the promotion, either directly or indirectly, of economic development and social change. Although it is very difficult to measure its short-term impact precisely, nobody would reject the notion that technological progress is changing the world at an incredible rate. The most obvious contribution is transport and communication, which have changed from the primitive means (such as horses, carriages, and hand-written letters) to advanced methods such as super jets, telephones, and faxes, as well as the increasingly efficient computer networks.

Chinese inventions—such as papermaking, gunpowder, movable-type printing, and the compass—have made enormous contributions to world civilization. For example, paper was introduced in China in the second century AD, reached Japan in the seventh century, and was then diffused westward to Central Asia in the eighth century. It reached North Africa in the tenth, Spain in the twelfth, and northern Europe in the thirteenth. Printing was invented in China in the eighth century AD and movable type in the eleventh century, but this technology only reached Europe in the fifteenth century. Another Chinese invention, gunpowder, was made in the ninth century, disseminated to the Arabs after a few hundred years and reached Europe in the fourteenth century. In recent centuries, however, China has lagged far behind Western nations in terms of technological innovation.

Before the early twentieth century, technological innovations had been contributed mainly by individual inventors or small-scale entrepreneurs. But now the great bulk of it—such as the invention of the space shuttle and the Internet, to list but two—has been conducted by prominent firms with substantial budgets, as well as by governments. As a result, the process of technological innovation becomes more complicated than ever before. Specifically, the technological and related products are positively related to capital stock of, and personnel engagement in, technological innovation. In addition, technological innovation is also related to the educational level, as the content of education changes over time to accommodate the growing stock of knowledge. There has been a proliferation of specialized intellectual disciplines to facilitate the absorption of knowledge and to promote its development through research.

After the founding of the PRC in 1949, China began to import advanced technology from the Soviet Union. Unfortunately, this process came to an abrupt halt following the worsening of Sino–Soviet relations in the late 1950s. Following its *rapprochement* with the US and Japan, China began the gradual importation of advanced technology from the capitalist nations. But economic relations between China and the technologically advanced nations did not improve significantly until the late 1970s when the new CCP and the state leaders tried to abandon the "leftist" ideology (of self-reliance and independence). By the early 1980s, China's production technology in the iron and steel industry was still that of the advanced nations in the 1950s; similarly, the scientific and technological level of the electronic industry was approximately 15 to 20 years behind advanced international standards (Liao 1982, p. 138).

It must be mentioned that some important advances in science and technology had been achieved during the pre-reform period. Notable technological milestones include the development of the atomic bomb in 1964 and of artificial satellites in 1970, which granted China a political seat with the superpowers. However, as this kind of technology has been controlled by the Science and Technology Commission for National Defense and guided by the State Council and the Central Military Commission, the transfer of military technology to social and economic uses is to some extent limited. Other sectors of the economy—such as China's metallurgical, coal, machine-building, oil, chemical, power, electric, and precision instrument industries—had acquired a stock of relatively advanced equipment. This provided the foundation for industrial modernization. Taken as a whole, however, the level of productivity still remained very low, as did the level of labor productivity.

In fact, Chinese policymakers clearly recognized the increasing role of technology in the Chinese economy and have also paid considerable attention to the acceleration of research and development (R&D). According to UNESCO (1986), during the 1980–85 period the R&D/GNP ratio of China was, although lower than that of the US, Japan, West Germany, the UK, and Switzerland (whose R&D/GNP ratios exceeded 2 percent), higher than that found in Pakistan, Indonesia, Thailand, and the Philippines, whose R&D/GNP ratios ranged between 1.0 percent and 0.4 percent, and very similar to that of Austria, Australia, Denmark, Italy, and South Korea, whose R&D ratios ranged between 1 percent and 1.2 percent. Since the mid-1980s, China has implemented a package of plans for the development of new technology, high technology, and traditional technology. These plans include, *inter alia* the:

- *"863" Plan*, which aims to track the frontiers of the high and new technologies and R&D;
- *Torchlight Plan*, which aims to promote the commercialization, industrialization, and internationalization of the high-tech products;
- *Climbing Plan*, which aims to organize the research and application of new and high technologies;
- *Spark Plan*, which aims to spread applicable technologies to small and medium-sized enterprises, TVEs, and other rural areas;
- *Harvest Plan*, which aims to popularize various kinds of technology contributing to agriculture, animal husbandry, and fishery.

However, many problems still exist in the Chinese science and technology sector, particularly during the 1990s. For example, China's R&D/GNP ratio declined rapidly alongside its GNP growth from the late 1980s to the mid-1990s. In 1995, China's expenditure on R&D was only 0.50 percent of GNP, compared with the R&D/GNP ratios of 0.93 percent in 1979 and 1.12 percent in 1986. Of course, the R&D/GNP ratio of China was much lower than that of many advanced countries,

nt, 1988), Japan (3.0 percent, 1991), France
JK (2.1 percent, 1991).[4] Nevertheless, since
een continuous increases of government
, with the R&D/GDP ratio growing at the
, _. year. In 2006, China's R&D/GDP ratio was
__ percent (NBS 2007). But, it was still far lower than that of
the advanced nations.

Creativity has been the most fundamental element in promoting, either directly or indirectly, economic development and social change. In China, there were great thinkers such as Confucius, Mencius, Laozi, and Zhuangzi. But these achievements go back the periods of the Spring and Autumn (770–476 BC) and the Warring States (475–221 BC), and there has not been a similar breakthrough within the past centuries. (A further discussion about this topic will be included in a section of Chapter 8.)

CULTURAL INFLUENCE

Culture is the living sum of symbols, meanings, habits, values, institutions, behaviors, and social artifacts that characterize a distinctive and identified human population group. It confers upon individuals an identity as members of some visible community; standards for relating to the environment, for identifying fellow members and strangers; and for distinguishing between what is important and what is unimportant to them. While others usually suggest more complicated compositions for a culture, we will only discuss three elements— ethnicity, language, and religion. Our consideration here is due to the concerns that: (1) "ethnicity" provides a genetic basis in which socio-economic behaviors between same and different groups of people can be differentiated easily; (2) "language" is an effective tool of communication; and (3) "religion" can provide the insights into the characteristics of culture.

For much of the Christian era, members of the ethnic majority in China have traditionally been referred to as the Han race. This may well be because of the relatively long period of social, political, economic, and military consolidation and stability enjoyed by the Chinese nation during the period of the Han dynasty (206 BC–AD 220). The term "Han," however, does not offer a full account of the cultural and ethnic origins of the Chinese people. It was, instead, an inclusive name for the various tribes that lived together on the Central China Plains well before the time of Christ. The trend over the ages was for many ethnic groups living adjacent to the Hua-Xia people to be assimilated at different times and to different degrees into what the Chinese have termed ultimately the Han culture. The original ethnic stock for this amalgam seems to have primarily included the Hua-Xia, Eastern Yi, Chu-Wu, and Baiyue groups. Other non-Han peoples were assimilated into the Han culture at different points in China's history.[5]

While the Han majority can be found throughout the country, China's ethnic minorities are scattered over vast areas of China. Historically, the total number of ethnic groups has never been fixed precisely. For example, in 1953, only 42 ethnic peoples were identified, while the number increased to 54 in 1964 and 56 in 1982. Geographically, most ethnic minorities are concentrated on the western inland areas, such as the Huis in Ningxia, the Ugyurs in Xinjiang, the Mongols in Inner Mongolia and Qinghai, and the Tibetans in Tibet and the surrounding areas. However, the ethnic Zhuang form the majority in the Guangxi Zhuang autonomous region in the southern coastal area.

During their histories, many ethnic groups have also established differing economic and cultural backgrounds. For example, the names of some ethnic groups can reveal certain information about their particular economic and cultural conditions, with a number of these highlighting a group's characteristic occupation. For example, in the language of the Lahu people, "Lahu" means "roasting tiger-meat on fire," from which it can be understood that the Lahu people used to live by hunting. This can also be witnessed by their neighbors in Southwest China, the Dai and Hani, who called themselves *Mushe* (meaning "hunters"). There is a small ethnic group called the *Oroqen* (a word that has two meanings: "people who rear tamed deer" and "people who live on the mountains") who live in the Greater and Lesser Xing'an Mountains in Northeast China. Another ethnic group, also living in Northeast China, call themselves the *Daur* (meaning "cultivator"), indicating that the Daur people engaged in agriculture during ancient times.

Since the dawn of China's Neolithic period, agriculture has been the economic mainstay of the Han people. In the embryonic stages of its ethnic development, the Han group lived primarily along the banks of China's major rivers. The area along the Yellow River, characterized by a semi-arid climate, with loose, fertile soil, was suitable for the growing of millet; while the tropical and semi-tropical climate of the areas along the Pearl and Yangtze rivers was good for rice production. Thus millet and rice could be said to be the staples that delineated early Han culture. While the Han culture continued to develop, commerce, industry, education, and government service were also viable livelihoods, as, for example, in the case of the transportation of food, clothing, and jewelry between the large walled cities and smaller, more remote towns. The non-Han minorities, such as the Tibetans, in western China, on the other hand, have traditionally had a mixed nomadic economy. The minority peoples in northeast China rely on either fishing and hunting or nomadism, while the Mongols have been mainly nomadic. The other minorities, such as the Uygurs in Xinjiang, have historically engaged in either agriculture or nomadism, but have supplemented their incomes through commerce.

China's linguistic system is understood in terms of its lexicon, grammar, syntax, phonetics, and so on. Chinese, the language spoke by the Han people—China's official language, which belongs to the Sino-Tibetan language family—is the most commonly used language in China and one of the most common languages in the world. Written Chinese emerged in its embryonic form of carved symbols approximately 6,000 years ago. The Chinese characters used today evolved from those used in bone and tortoise shell inscriptions more than 3,000 years ago, and the bronze inscriptions produced soon after. Drawn figures were gradually reduced to patterned strokes, pictographs were reduced to symbols, and, eventually, the complicated became simplified. Earlier pictographs and ideographs were joined by pictophonetic characters. Chinese is monosyllable. The vast majority of Chinese characters used today are composed of an ideogrammatic portion on the left and the phonetic on the right.[6]

In addition to Chinese, a number of other languages are also used regionally and locally in China. Specifically, 23 of these languages have taken written forms. Five linguistic systems are represented: 29 languages, including Zhuang, Dai, Tibetan, Yi, Miao, and Yao, belong to the Han-Tibetan language family; 17 languages, including Uygur, Kazak, Mongolian, and Korean, come under the Altaian language family; three languages, the Va, Deang, and Blang, originate from the South Asian language family; and Gaoshan is an Austronesian language. The Jing language has yet to be classified typologically. The main non-Han Chinese languages used in China are: Zhuang (spoken) in most parts of Guangxi and some parts of Guangdong, Yunnan, and Guizhou; Ugyur (spoken and written) in Xinjiang and some parts of Qinghai; Tibetan (spoken and written) in Tibet and the surrounding areas; Mongolian (spoken and written) in Inner Mongolia, Qinghai, and the surrounding areas; Yi (spoken) in some parts of Sichuan, Yunnan, Guizhou, and Guangxi provinces; and English (spoken and written) in Hong Kong and so on.

Although Mandarin is standardized nationwide as *putonghua*, each region speaks its own local version, usually reflecting influence from the native dialect of the area. Chinese dialects are spoken in three-quarters of the country by two-thirds of the population throughout China. Generally, these dialects can be classified into six groups: Xiang, Gan, Kejia, Wu, Min, and Cantonese (Yue). These dialects have the following features:

- The Xiang dialect (in Hunan area) and the Gan dialect (in Jiangxi area) each has six tones. In some areas such as Changsha and Nanchang, these dialects do not distinguish between the constants l- and n-.

- The Kejia dialect, mostly found in Guangdong, Taiwan, and other scattered areas in Southeast Asia, also has six tones.
- The Wu dialects are mostly spoken in Shanghai, Jiangsu, and Zhejiang provinces. The Suzhou dialect of Jiangsu province, representing the northern Wu, has seven tones; the Wenzhou dialect of Zhejiang province, treated as the southern Wu, has eight tones; and the Shanghai dialect has five tones.
- The Min dialects are spoken widely in Fujian, Taiwan, Hainan, and many areas of Southeast Asia, including Singapore and the Philippines. The Min group includes Northern and Southern Min. While the Northern Min is represented by Fuzhou, the Southern Min dialect, which has seven tones, is mostly spoken in eastern Fujian and most parts of the Taiwan area. Southern and Northern Min dialects are for the most part mutually unintelligible.
- Cantonese (Yue), with a total of nine tones, which is more than any other dialect, is the main dialect of Guangdong, Hong Kong, Macau, and many overseas Chinese communities.

The main unifying force of China's many diverse dialects is the shared written system. It is generally believed that the unified Chinese characters used by people speaking different dialects make it possible for the central government to maintain control effectively over a vast size of territory. However, achieving mastery of the many thousands of Chinese characters is a very long and time-consuming process. This strengthened Chinese ethnocentrism, encouraged self-satisfaction, and inhibited the intellectuals' deviance or curiosities. On the other hand, the written Chinese is not a wide open door through which the mass peasants gain access to truth and knowledge; rather, all too often it is the stumbling block for their progresses.

Founded by Kongzi or Confucius (551–479 BC), Confucianism was reputed to have served as the basis of the traditional Chinese culture. *Lunyu* (Analects of Confucius) records the saying and deeds of Confucius and his disciples. It covers a wide range of subjects, ranging from politics, philosophy, literature and art, to education and moral cultivation. With only 12,000 characters, it is terse but comprehensive, rich yet profound; as the major classic of Confucianism as well as the most authoritative, it has influenced the Chinese society for over 2,000 years. Its ideas have taken such firm root in China that all Chinese—both Han and non-Han ethnicities—have been more or less influenced by it. Since the Han dynasty, every ruler has had to pay at least some heed to this, and people also expected their ruler to act accordingly in China. Confucian philosophy concerning the relationship between politics and morality serves as the basis of the Confucian school's emphasis on moral education. This can be found in the Analects of Confucius: "Regulated by the edicts and punishments, the people will know only how to stay away out of trouble, but will not have a sense of shame. Guided by virtues and the rites, they will not only have a sense of shame, but also know how to correct their mistakes of their own accord." This idea also represented the distinguishing feature of the Oriental cultural realm under the influence of Confucianism.

Taoism originated from sorcery, the pursuit of immortality, and other supernatural beliefs that were present in ancient China. Taoists look to the philosopher Laozi (or Lao Tzu, born in about 600 BC) as their great leader, and take his work *The Classic of the Way and Its Power* ("Daode Jing" or "Tao Te Ching") as their canon. Mystifying the philosophical concept of "Dao" or "Tao" (the way, or path), they posit that man could become one with the "Dao" through self-cultivation and can thereby achieve immortality. As an escape from Confucianism, Taoism has been promoted by a group of scholars working against the overnice ritualism and detailed prescriptions of Classical texts. It has also denoted the common people's belief in certain traditional super-institutions. Applying the idea of balance in all things, Taoism argues that human moral ideas are the reflection of human depravity, that the idea of filial piety springs from the fact of impiety, that the Confucian statement of the rules of propriety is really a reflection of the world's moral disorder. Later, Taoism developed in two directions. The first one, represented by Zhuangzi (*c.* 369—295 BC), resulted in so-called nihilism. The second one, with the Tao as the basis of proprieties and laws, led to the founding of the Legalist school.

For much of the past 2,500 years, Confucianism and Taoism have had a substantial influence on China's political and economic behaviors. The ethical beliefs of Confucianism have remained consistently within the bounds of a set of orthodox principles governing interpersonal relationships in China. They have been applied officially to all strata of society and include loyalty, filial piety, benevolence, righteousness, love, faith, harmony, and peace. As a result, China has developed a different culture in economic development than is found in the rest of the world, in response to its own particular environment and social conditions (see Chapter 8 for an indepth analysis).

Through the entire course of Chinese history, Chinese culture has been reconstructed as the result of external influences. Among the first, and the most important is the importation of Buddhism from India in the first century BC. At the heart of Buddhism there are Four Noble Truths: (1) existence is suffering; (2) suffering has a cause, namely craving and attachment; (3) there is a cessation of suffering, which is Nirvana; and (4) there is a path to the cessation of suffering, which includes the Noble Eightfold Path—that is, right view, right intention, right speech, right action, right livelihood, right effort, right mindfulness, and right concentration. Nirvana is the ultimate goal of Buddhism. It represents the extinction of all cravings and the final release from sufferings. To the extent that such an ideal reflects the thinking of the mass of people, a Buddhist society's values would be considered antithetical to goals such as acquisition, achievement, or affluence. Buddhism became increasingly popular after the fourth century AD and has now been a Chinese religion and an important part of Chinese culture. Tibetan Buddhism, or Lamaism as it is sometimes called, is founded primarily in Tibet and Mongolia. One of the tenets of Buddhism is that life is painful and that it is not limited to the mortal span with which we are familiar.

In the mid-seventh century, Muslim Arab, and Persian merchants came overland through Central Asia to northwest China and by sea to Guangdong and other southeastern ports, bringing with them the Islamic faith. Christian belief was first introduced to China approximately 1,000 years ago. During the Ming (AD 1368–1644) and the Qing (1644–1911) dynasties, a large number of Christian missionaries began to arrive in China. They brought not only their religion but also new concepts of science and technology. Today, China is a country that displays considerable religious diversity. Apart from the Protestants and Roman Catholics, who are scattered across the nation, most of the other religious followers have either a geographical or ethnic orientation in China. Most Han people traditionally engage in folk religious practices, usually mixed with elements from Confucianism, Taoism, and Buddhism. The Hui, Uygur, Kazak, Kirgiz, Tatar, Ozbek, Tajik, Dongxiang, Salar, and Bonan people, mostly in the area of northwest China, adhere to Islamic culture. The Tibetans, Mongols, Lhoba, Moinba, Tu, and Yugur follow a creed of Tibetan Buddhism (also known as Lamaism); whereas the Blang and Deang in Southwest China favor Theravada Buddhism. The minorities of Southwest China such as the Dai tend to be adherents of the Hinayana school of Buddhism. Some minorities in Jilin and Heilongjinag provinces subscribe to shamanism, while other ethnic groups living in the valleys of the southwestern mountain ranges embrace animist beliefs.

ENDNOTES

1   This is calculated as $1/(1 - (0.03 - 0.01) - 1 \approx 0.0204$.
2   Data source: NBS (2002). According to Du (1994, p. 88), the proportion of the aged population in China will increase steadily to 8.1 percent in 2010, 10.9 percent in 2020, 14.7 percent in 2030, 19.8 percent in 2040, and 20.9 percent in 2050.
3   The expenditure on R&D refers to all actual expenditure made for R&D (fundamental research, applied research, and experimental development).
4   Data sources: UNESCO (1995, tab. 5) and Guo (2009a).

5   They are, for example, the Huns (Xiongnu) and Xianbei between the third
    and fifth century AD, the Eastern Hu and the Jurchens (ancestors of the
    Manchus) from the tenth through to the early thirteenth century, and the
    Manchus through their conquest of China in the seventeenth century.

6   For example, the Chinese character for the tree that produces tung oil is
    composed of an ideogram on the left representing a tree, and a phonogram on
    the right indicating that the word should be pronounced *tong* (as would this
    phonetic element if it were an independent character).

CHAPTER FIVE

POLITICAL AND ECONOMIC SYSTEMS

Ding—A symbol of imperial power in ancient China

Source: http://en.wikipedia.org
Note: Permission is granted to copy, distribute, and/or modify this document under the terms of the GNU Free Documentation License, Version 1.3 or any later version published by the Free Software Foundation; with no Invariant Sections, no Front-Cover Texts, and no Back-Cover Texts. A copy of the license is included in the section entitled "GNU Free Documentation License."

The advocates of new institutional economics recognize that a good market economy requires "getting institutions right" (Coase 1992; North 1997; Williamson 1994). The institutional economists thus regard the conventional wisdom of transition focusing on stabilization, liberalization, and privatization as inadequate, because it overlooks the important institutional dimension. Standing in marked contrast with the failures of some former socialist economies, which were to some extent based on a "blueprint" or "recipe" from Western advisors, has been the enormous success of China, through its own political and economic transitions. However, China's political system has increasingly proven inadequate in dealing with the complicated and sometimes contradictory needs of the Chinese economy and society . . .

> Bianque stood looking at Duke Huang of Cai for a while and spoke, "Your Majesty is suffering from an ailment, which now remains in between the skin and the muscles. But it may get worse without treatment." "I am not at all indisposed," replied the Duke complacently. When Bianque left, the Duke remarked, "It is the medical man's usual practice to pass a healthy person as a sick man in order to show his brilliance." Ten days later, when Bianque saw the Duke, he pointed out: "The ailment has developed into the muscles. It will go from bad to worse if no treatment is conducted." To this the ruler showed a greater displeasure than before. Another 10 days went by. On seeing the Duke again, Bianque warned him that the illness had gone into the stomach and the intestines and that unless an immediate treatment be given, it would go on worsening. Again the Duke looked angrier. After a third 10 days, when Bianque saw the Duke, he simply turned round and went away . . . (*to be continued*)[1]
>
> —*Hanfeizi* (*c.* 280–233 BC)

PARTY VERSUS STATE

China's current constitution, first adopted by the National People's Congress (NPC) in 1982 and subsequently amended, is the country's fourth and it restored the office of Head of State. The State Council is the official government of China. It initiates legislation and controls the civil service. The State Council is indirectly elected by the NPC, which assembles in plenary every year to scrutinize and ratify its decisions on domestic and foreign affairs. The Chinese People's Political Consultative Congress (CPPCC)—an institution similar to the Senate in the US—consists of representatives from the Chinese Communist Party (CCP), several democratic parties, democrats with no party affiliations, various people's organizations and ethnic groups, and other specially invited individuals. The primary functions of the CPPCC are to conduct political consultations and democratic supervisions, and to discuss and manage state affairs.

The 3,000 deputies that attend the NPC are elected indirectly every five years by the People's Congresses of provinces, autonomous regions, municipalities under central government, and by the People's Liberation Army (PLA). The supreme legislative organ of China, the NPC holds regular (annual) meetings in the Great Hall of the People in Beijing to discuss state affairs, to approve those whom are recommended by the Chinese Communist Party Central Committee (CCPCC) as central government officials, and to issue laws and regulations. In addition to indirectly electing the State Council, the NPC can also dismiss the holders of the top offices of State. The Standing Committee of the NPC is empowered to modify legislation between plenary sessions and carry out the daily work of the NPC on a more permanent basis. In practice, although its scrutiny role has been enhanced in recent years and unanimous votes have become less frequent, the independent power of the NPC remains limited.[2]

Provincial government comprises 22 provinces, five autonomous regions, four municipalities under central government (Beijing, Chongqing, Shanghai, and Tianjin), and two special administrative regions (SARs)—Hong Kong and Macau—which returned to China in 1997 and 1999, respectively. It was agreed on handover that the existing political and economic systems that prevailed prior to these dates would be maintained for 50 years. Governments at this level (with the exception of the SARs) are indirectly elected for five years at plenaries of their respective People's Congresses. Sub-provincial government comprises a three-level administrative network of prefectures, cities and counties, and townships and districts. Their governments are indirectly elected for three years by their respective People's Congresses.

In addition, there are also systems of governance that operate beneath the various levels of state administration described above. These are the village committees (*cunweihui*) in rural areas and the resident committees (*juweihui*) in urban areas. The village committees deal with all administrative matters, including tax collection, budgets, public services, order, welfare, and dispute resolution. In contrast to their attitude with regard to levels of government that are considered part of the state, the authorities have shown some willingness over the past two decades to countenance direct elections to these committees. There have been attempts to introduce direct elections to village committees. These innovations were part of wider efforts to restore some form of governance at village level. Urban resident committees usually cover regions with a size ranging from 100 to over 1,000 households. Reformers have suggested that urban electoral reform should begin with direct elections.

Although there are other political organizations in China, the only organization that matters is the CCP. Some 2,000 CCP delegates are elected to the National Congress of the CCP, which is held every five years. The National Congress elects the members and alternative members of the CCPCC, which normally sits once a year. The current (17th) CCPCC, which was elected in 2007, is composed of 371 members and hundreds more alternative members. The Central Committee for Discipline Inspection (CCDI) is also elected at this Congress. Immediately after the closing ceremony of the National Congress, the CCPCC members indirectly elect, in addition to the Central Military Commission, the General Secretary, members of the Politburo and its Standing Committee, and the Secretariat (see Figure 5.1). The Politburo and particularly the smaller Standing Committee of the Politburo are where the overall policy of the Chinese government is really decided.

The CCP has been virtually the most important power body in China and holds real political power in China's *de facto* one-party state.

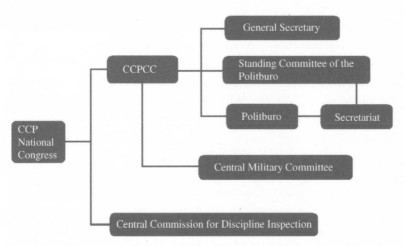

Note: CCP = Chinese Communist Party; CCPCC = Chinese Communist Party Central Committee

Figure 5.1 Structure of the Communist Party of China

Party organizations run in parallel to those of the government at all levels. The CCP's structure is characterized by "democratic centralism" (*minzhu jizhong*), a system whereby the individual party member is subordinate to the organization, and where minority groups or opinions are subordinate to the wishes of the majority, embodied by the CCPCC. At the bottom of this pyramid are "primary party organizations" in workplaces and villages. The overwhelming majority of delegates to the NPC are party members. CCP membership remains essential for a successful career, particularly in the public sector. Party membership now stands at nearly 80 million, which continues to increase.

Indeed, the CCP's "three representatives" theory states clearly that the CCP is no longer the single representative of poor, working-class people; rather, it has also been the representative of the economic and cultural elites in China. By openly proclaiming itself a party of the "economic elite" that has benefited from its free market agenda, the CCP has been hoping to consolidate a reliable base of support for its continued rule. With its pro-growth polices, its ban on independent trade unions and its low environmental standards, the CCP has created an advantageous atmosphere for the economic elite to make money. Many successful entrepreneurs have also been party members. Policies favor the rich and business so much that China's economic program, in the words of one Western ambassador, resembles "the dream of the American Republican Party."

STATE AND MARKET

In traditional socialist countries, economic development is realized mainly through a plan worked out by the central planning authorities. The plan, however, is a mental construct that may or may not correctly reflect the objective requirements of economic development. If the plan is correct, economic development is smooth; if it is incorrect, not only is it of no help—it may even lead to stagnation and decline. Obviously this has been proven in China's economic sphere, especially during the pre-reform period.

During the early 1950s, the transformation of private ownership of the means of production to public ownership and the establishment of a powerful socialist sector paved an effective way for planned development of the national economy. During the first Five-Year Plan (1953–57), much attention was paid to industrial construction, especially in heavy industry. At the same time, the socialist transformation of agriculture, handicrafts, and capitalist industry and commerce was effectively carried out. In line with these goals, 156 key projects and other items were arranged with the guidance of the Soviet Union. The first Five-Year Plan was generally thought by the PRC's central planners and economists to be very successful because all scheduled targets were fully met.

Facing the economic difficulties during the late 1950s and the early 1960s, the CCPCC and the State Council advanced a policy entitled "readjustment, consolidation, filling-out, and raising standards" (*tiaozheng, gonggu, chongshi, tigao*). The production targets for heavy industry were reduced and investment in capital construction was cut back. This investment rate, which had risen to as high as 39.9 percent in 1960, was adjusted sharply downward, reaching only 10.4 percent by 1962. The enterprises with high production costs and large losses were closed or switched to other products. With the adjustments, the economy rapidly returned to normal. In contrast to the first Five-Year Plan and the readjustment period (1963–65), the years 1958–60 provided a typical case of errors in planning, which resulted in serious economic imbalances. During this period, the Great Leap Forward movement was effectively launched by the establishment of a series of high targets within a given period, most of which, however, were incapable of being fulfilled due to the limitation of resources and production capacities. To accomplish its ambitious target for an overnight entrance to the "communist heaven," large quantities of raw materials and the labor force were diverted toward heavy industry, while, in contrast, the development of agriculture and light industry received less attention. This situation lasted until 1960 when the serious imbalances between accumulation and consumption and between heavy industry on the one hand and agriculture and light industry on the other occurred suddenly. Despite this profound lesson, similar problems arose again thereafter.

In the Third Plenum of the 11th Chinese Communist Party Central Committee (CCPCC), held on December 18, 1978, Deng Xiaoping and his senior supporters took decisive control of the CCPCC. This ended what has been described as two years of uncertainty and indecisive strategy and policy following the death of Mao Zedong. The Third Plenum of the 11th CCPCC, which was held in December 1978, marked a major turning point in China's reform and development. After a decade of turmoil brought about by the Cultural Revolution (1966–76), the new direction set at this meeting was toward economic development and away from class struggle. The course was laid for the CCP to move the world's most populous nation toward the ambitious targets of the Four Modernizations in the sectors of industry, agriculture, science and technology, and national defense.

In brief, the institutional evolution in the Chinese economy since 1978 has followed a gradual path and may be outlined in six phases listed below:

1. a centrally planned economy (before 1978);
2. an economy regulated mainly by planning and supplementation by the market (1978–84);
3. a commodity economy with a plan (1985–87);
4. a combination of planned and market economies (1988–91);
5. a socialist market economy with *state* ownership as the main form (1992–97);
6. a socialist market economy with *public* ownership as the main form of ownership (from 1998 onwards).

Generally, Phase 3 was known to be based loosely on the Hungarian model of market socialism. Nevertheless, the state continued to own the bulk of large and medium-sized enterprises and to regulate the production and pricing of a number of strategic commodities, but the market mechanism was permitted to play an increasing role in the pricing and allocation of goods and services, and in the allocation and remuneration of labor in some non-strategic sectors. In the ideological struggles between the radical reformers and the conservatives, there was a new term, "socialist commodity economy," used between 1988 and 1989, but this was replaced by Phase 4 ("a combination of planned and market economies") immediately after the Tiananmen Square incident of May–June 1989. Nevertheless, Phase 4 was extremely important insofar as it legitimated the abolition of the traditional mechanisms of the central planning system in favor of the introduction of market regulation.

During the 1980s, China's reform and open-door policy resulted in an increase in economic prosperity, but it also led to some political and social instability. This can be witnessed by the CCP's "anti-spiritual pollution" and "anti-bourgeois liberalization" campaigns, which were launched in 1983 and 1987, respectively. This kind of political disequilibria between the CCP conservatives and intellectuals reached its high point in 1989, and, in combination with other factors such as high inflation and official corruption, eventually became a leading cause of students' protests against the CCP and central government during May–June 1989. As soon as the aftermath of the Tiananmen incident had subsided, there was a shift of power in economic decision-making from the reformers to the conservatives. This led to a temporary brake being placed on China's economic reforms and also on its rates of economic growth.

At the beginning of the 1990s the socialist camp in Eastern Europe and the former Soviet Union both suffered sudden collapses. China's immediate reaction to the collapse of these communist regimes was a policy of re-centralization, but the CCP soon realized that its legitimacy could be sustained only through economic growth brought about by further reforms. Amid the political deadlock between the reformers and conservatives concerning how to combine the planned and market economic systems, Deng Xiaoping made his now famous southern tour to the province of Guangdong in early 1992. Drawing on regional support for continued reforms, Deng's visit tipped the political balance in the CCPCC and the central government. This resulted in China's official declaration in October 1992 of its intention to build a "socialist market economy," as well as a calling for faster reforms and economic development.

In the early 1990s, some of the policies applied to the coastal special economic zones (SEZs) were extended to a list of inland regions and cities along the Yangtze River and, as a result of the normalization of China's diplomatic relations with the former USSR, to the border cities and towns adjacent to Russia and other neighboring countries. Furthermore, many inland cities, which did not qualify for this special treatment, established numerous economic and technological development zones inside their regions. It is noteworthy that the wide-ranging pro-development reforms during these years brought about not only high economic growth, but also the double-digit inflationary pressures that occurred in 1993. Facing an overheating economy, the Chinese government announced a series of banking and financial reforms in 1994, which were aimed at eliminating some of the structural inefficiencies in the financial sector.

China's ambitious agenda geared toward transforming the Chinese economy into a market-oriented one was unveiled as early as 1992, when Deng Xiaoping's Southern Speech eventually had an influence on China's decision makers. On November 14, 1993, a formal document entitled "Decision of the CCPCC on Several Issues Concerning the Establishment of a Socialist Market Economic Structure" was finally approved by the Third Plenum of the 14th CCPCC. The aim of the decision was that the government should withdraw from direct involvement in enterprise management. Instead, "Government functions in economic management consist mainly of devising and implementing macroeconomic control policies, appropriate construction of infrastructure facilities, and creation of a favorable environment for economic development" (Article 16). The Plenum also declared that "the government shall take significant steps in the reform of taxation, financing, investment and planning systems, and establish a mechanism in which planning, banking, and public finance coordinate and mutually check each other while strengthening the overall coordination of economic operations" (Article 17).

The 15th National Congress of the CCP, held in 1997, witnessed a historic breakthrough in terms of the reform of the ownership structure of the national economy. The three aspects of adjustment were: (1) to reduce the scope of the state sector and to withdraw state capital from industries that were considered nonessential to the national economy; (2) to seek various forms for materializing public ownership that can generally promote the growth of productive forces and to develop diverse forms of public ownership; and (3) to encourage the development of nonpublic sectors of the economy such as the individual business sector and the private sector, and to make them important components of a socialist market economy (Wu 2005, p. 86). In September 2003, as the "Decision on Issues Regarding the Improvement of the Socialist Market Economic System" was adopted by the Third Plenary Session of the 16th CCPCC, it indicated that China's economic, social, and political reforms will continue to be advanced comprehensively in the years to come.

MARKET-ORIENTED REFORM

The ultimate goal of any economic system is the allocation of scarce resources among competing factions. To accomplish this goal, the economic system must deal explicitly with the supply and demand of goods and services, as well as the interaction between the two. From the founding of the PRC in 1949, the Chinese government had uneasily followed the Soviet Union and adopted a centrally planned economy (CPE). Generally, this kind of planning system has the following problems. First of all, it makes almost all productive enterprises subordinate to administrative organs. To a large extent, this neglects the economic independence of the enterprises and thereby leads to the neglect of their material interests and responsibilities, blunting the levels of initiative and enthusiasm. Second, the system involves excessive command planning from above and is overly rigid. So long as the enterprises meet their stipulated targets, they are considered to have performed satisfactorily—regardless of whether or not its products satisfy social needs.

Since a socialist economy is rigorously directed by state planning, as soon as errors occur in the plan, this will have an effect on every economic activity. China bore witness to this point by its experience and lessons. Theoretically, it is essential to make a "perfect" plan for the healthy operation of the economy. However, it is almost impossible for the state planners to accurately manage a balance between social production and social needs, and efficiently distribute the scarce resources even with the use of the sophisticated computers. In fact, because of information constraints and asymmetries the central planners could never obtain complete and accurate information on economic activities from which to formulate plans. Furthermore, the centrally planned system also triggered a number of other problems. For example, as wages were fixed, workers had no incentive to work once they had reached the factory's output quota. Any extra production might have led to the increase of the following year's quota while the level of salaries would remain unchanged. Factory managers and government planners frequently bargained over work targets, funds, and material supplies allocated to the factory. Usually, government agencies allocated less than managers requested so managers would, in turn, request more than they needed; when bargaining over the production, the managers, however, proposed a smaller quota than they were able to finish, and so they were usually ordered to fulfill a larger quota than requested.

China's decentralization of its mandatory planning system and the introduction of market mechanisms, which began in 1978, first focused on a gradual transition from the people's commune system (PCS) to the household responsibility system (HRS) under which farmers were free to decide what and how to produce in their contracted farmlands and, having fulfilled the state's production quotas, were permitted both to sell the excess of their produce on the free market and also to pursue some non-agricultural activities. In 1984, when urban reform was implemented, China aimed to regulate industrial production through the operation of market forces. In a similar manner to the system adopted in the agricultural sector, after fulfilling their output quotas, enterprises could make profits by selling their excess products at free or floating prices. It is worthwhile noting that the above efforts resulted inevitably in dual prices for commodities during the transition period, and had both positive and negative effects.

China's economic reform has followed a double-track system in which the reform was first implemented in agricultural products and thereafter spread slowly to consumer goods and intermediate goods. In each case, a free market in which the price was subject to the market regulations developed in parallel with a controlled market in which the price was kept almost unchanged at an officially fixed level. Because the price was higher in the market-regulated track than in the state-controlled track, the free market supply grew rapidly, and its share of total output rose steadily. Meanwhile, the planned price rose incrementally until it approached the market price where there was a narrowing of the gap between supply and demand. The dual-pricing system provided opportunities for people who had access to state-controlled goods and materials to make large profits by buying them at an officially fixed low price and reselling them at a market-based price, which often led to unequal competition as well as official corruption. Nevertheless, this dual market created various distortions and speculative transactions.

By the end of 1986, the number of key industrial products under the direct control of the State Planning Commission (SPC) had fallen from 120 to 60; accordingly, the share of industrial production fell from 40 percent to 20 percent; the number of commodities and materials distributed by the state (that is, *tongpei wuzhi*) dropped from 250 to 20, and the number of goods controlled by the Ministry of Commerce (MOC) decreased from 188 to 25; the share of prices which were "free" or "floating" increased to about 65 percent in agriculture and supplementary products, 55 percent of consumer goods and 40 percent of production materials (State Council 1988, p. 198). During the 1980s and the early 1990s this double-track system extended across almost every sphere of the Chinese economy, from agriculture, industry, commerce, transportation, post and telecommunications, health care and education. By the late 1990s, the dual-pricing system had deregulated more than 90 percent of retail prices and agricultural and intermediate product prices, and removed the mandatory plans of a large number of products, including fuel and raw materials.

China's commitment to the creation of a market-oriented economy has been the central plank of its program of economic reform, and considerable progress toward this end has been achieved since 1978, through the gradual withdrawal of the government from the allocation, pricing, and distribution of goods. To date the reforms introduced have achieved remarkable results. Particularly praiseworthy are the facts that the Chinese-type reforms have avoided the collapse in output characteristic of transitions in other former CPEs and generated unprecedented increases in the level of living standards across the country. Over the course of the past few decades, China has successfully implemented a stable economic reform and opened up to the outside world, and, in particular, achieved a faster economic growth than any other socialist or former socialist country in the world.

ENTERPRISE MANAGEMENT

After the founding of the PRC, the Chinese government reformed the ownership of land (*tugai*) and distributed the cultivated land proportionally among farmers. As a result, the farmers' incentives to work increased significantly. However, the new leadership only took this land reform as a provisional measure and did not consider it to be proper for a socialist economy. In the second half of the 1950s, China began to transform its private ownership of land. By 1958, the people's commune system (PCS) had been adopted as a universal form of agricultural production throughout mainland China. About 150 million rural households were grouped into five million production teams that, in turn, were organized nationwide into 50,000 people's communes (Minami 1994, p. 77).

Under the PCS, land was owned collectively and the output was distributed to each household according to the work points (*gongfen*). The state purchased a major share of the grain output and distributed it to the non-agricultural population through government agencies. For much of the pre-reform period, the independent accounting unit was the production team. In the Great Leap Forward and the high tide of the Cultural Revolution, the production brigades (usually including several production teams) and even the people's communes (usually including several production brigades) were selected as independent accounting units in some "advanced" areas where peasants were persuaded to pool their resources. Naturally, the PCS generally has been known to provide disincentives for the farmers to work harder.

The PCS lasted for more than 20 years before the Chinese government began to introduce a household-based and production-related responsibility system—the household responsibility system (HRS)—in the early 1980s. Under the HRS each household may be able to sign a contract with the local government to obtain a certain amount of arable land and production equipment depending on the number of rural population in each family. As long as the household completes its quota of products to the state, it can decide freely what to produce and how to sell. Although land is still owned by the state, the HRS and the PCS are definitely different from each other.

In the rural sector, although the system of collective ownership of land has been retained, farmers' rights and responsibilities are now clearer since the leasing period is long (15 years for the initial stage with an extension of a further 30 years). Before the reform, farmers had to sell to the government all the remaining gains (which was seen as being vital to the large Chinese population at that time) and other important agricultural products at a very low price. Following the reforms, the farmers could sell part of their products in the market at market prices. The policies behind rural price reform were thereafter introduced as part of many urban sector reforms during the 1980s.

The HRS has been recognized as a success. However, this system has also encountered some problems since the 1990s, especially since the late 1990s. This can be witnessed by the increasingly wider gaps between the rural and urban incomes during the 1990s and the 2000s. In brief, there have been two shortcomings for the HRS. First, since the management of agricultural production has been restricted within each household (note that the average size of the Chinese rural household has been reduced substantially as a result of the birth control policy implemented during the past decades), large-scale, mechanically based modern agriculture cannot be easily realized and, consequently, labor productivity has not been able to rise. Second, and as a result of the emigration of rural laborers into urban areas, a certain amount of arable land has been abandoned. In order to solve these problems, Chinese policymakers have brought forward two countermeasures: (1) within three years, starting from 2004, agricultural tax, which had been applied since 1958, was abolished; and (2) a *de facto* land privatization scheme, called "land circulation" (*tudi liuzhuan*) for rural areas, was proposed at the Third Plenum of the 17th CCPCC in October 2008.

China's industrial organization experienced a period of over centralization and then a period of decentralization. In much of the pre-reform period, China's industrial organization was implemented via a centrally planned system that offered the advantages of rapid structural transformation through direct and strong government participation and large-scale mobilization of resources to priority sectors. Such a system enabled the industrial sector to grow at highly creditable rates between 1953 and 1978. The advantages of rapid structural change under a centrally planned system, however, were soon outweighed by the problems of low efficiency, slow technological progress, sectoral imbalances, and sharp annual fluctuations in growth rates.

In general, the state-owned enterprises (SOEs) were established to serve five essential roles in the Chinese economy: (1) in many cases they had led to improved efficiency and increased technological competitiveness; (2) they had generally taken a more socially responsible attitude than the purely private enterprises; (3) they had helped to prevent oligopolistic collusion by refusing to collude; (4) they had helped the government to pursue its regional policy by shifting the investment to the poor west of the country; and (5) they had been used by the government as a means of managing aggregate demand to enable it to operate its counter-cyclical policy. Closely copying the Soviet prototype, the Chinese SOEs followed a "unified supply and unified collection" system in which the state supplied all inputs (such as labor, funds, raw material, power supply, and so on) necessary to execute production targets and claimed all output and financial revenues.

The main substantive difference between the collectively owned enterprises (COEs) and the SOEs lies in the extent of government control that is exerted over the organizations. The SOEs serve, to some extent, as the concrete manifestation of the socialist principle of the public ownership of the means of production by the whole population. Local governments are responsible for the provision of inputs to the COEs within their jurisdiction and conversely have first, if not sole claim to their output and revenues. Usually, the COEs are classified into two parts: urban COEs are directly controlled by local governments and subjected to state plans; rural COEs are fully under the jurisdiction of the township and village government units.

Obviously, the private, shareholding or other enterprises (PSEs) were the freest to decide on investment, labor, output and pricing, and, above all, were the most market-oriented. China's PSEs practically ceased to exist from 1958, when the socialist transformation of national capitalist industry was completed, to 1979 when the Chinese government made the decision to reform. During this reform era, the PSEs experienced a recovery between 1978–88, a period of consolidation during 1989–91, and have enjoyed a mushrooming since 1992. The foreign-invested enterprises (FIEs) mainly comprise joint ventures and wholly foreign-owned enterprises. Like the PSEs, the FIEs have also grown rapidly since the early 1980s, as a result of the dramatic inflows of foreign capital into China.

Since 1978, industrial reforms in China have sought to improve the enterprise incentive systems, to utilize indirect economic levers (price, tax, interest rate, credit, banking, and the rest) to regulate industrial production, to endow enterprises with greater relative decision-making autonomy, and, above all, to compel enterprises to operate according to market regulations. The positive effects of reform on industrial performance are evident from the dramatic industrial growth that was observed during the reform period. The dynamism of the industrialization may be attributed to a variety of reform measures. One such measure was the shift in sectoral priorities within industry, which allowed a greater share of resources to be diverted away from the input- and capital-intensive producer goods industries toward the more efficient and profitable consumer goods industries. Another measure was the lifting of previous restrictions on the development of the non-state sectors and the policy of promoting a diversified ownership structure. This has led to the explosive growth of the non-state sectors, which are acting increasingly as the engine of industrial development, particularly since the early 1990s when China

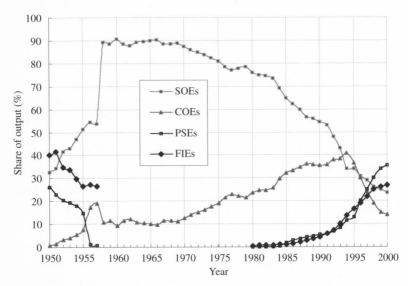

Notes: SOEs = state-owned enterprises; COEs = collectively owned enterprises; PSEs = private, share-holding or other enterprise; FIEs = foreign (Taiwan, Hong Kong and Macau) invested enterprises.

Figure 5.2   Shares of industrial output by ownership

formally tried to transform its economy to a socialist market system. From 1978 to 2000, the shares of industrial output produced by the SOEs, COEs, PSEs, and FIEs changed greatly, with the gross value of industrial output (GVIO) growing much slower in the SOEs than in the COEs, PSEs, and FIEs. It is particularly noteworthy that the SOEs' share in GVIO first began to rank after the PSEs and FIEs in 1997 and 1998, respectively (see Figure 5.2).

The substantial reform of the state industrial organization began in 1984 when the CCPCC and the central government decided to shift the emphasis of reforms from the agricultural sector to the non-agricultural sectors. On May 10, 1984, the State Council issued the "Provisional Regulations on the Enlargement of Autonomy of State-owned Industrial Enterprises," which outlines 10 specific decision-making powers to be enjoyed by enterprises. The "invigoration" of large and medium-sized SOEs and the application of indirect means to regulate

SOEs were adopted as policy in the State Council's governmental report to the Fourth Session of the Sixth NPC on March 25, 1986. In December, the "Bankruptcy Law Concerning the State Enterprises" was adopted by the NPC. However, the Bankruptcy Law was not effectively applied until the early 1990s due to fears of unemployment and social instability as China does not have a complete social security system.

Following Deng Xiaoping's call for faster economic growth and reform, after 1992 the government began to accelerate and intensify market-oriented reforms. Industrial reform was focused on the issue of property right reform by granting more autonomy to the SOEs. In June 1992, the State Commission for Restructuring the Economic Systems (SCRES), the State Planning Commission (SPC), the Ministry of Finance (MOF), the People's Bank of China (PBC), and the Production Office of State Council jointly issued the "Provisional Regulations on Joint-Stock Companies" to govern the formation of shareholding companies. The regulations cover the standardization of joint stock companies, their accounting system, financial management, taxation and auditing, as well as labor and wage systems. This was followed by the State Council's "Regulations on the Transformation of the Operating Mechanisms of State-owned Industrial Enterprises" on July 22, 1992, which codified the independent decision-making powers of the SOEs in 14 key areas (including production, investment, labor, marketing, independent profit and loss accounting, assets, mergers, closures, bankruptcy, and so on).

Since the formal adoption in 1993 of Deng Xiaoping's theory on the construction of a socialist market economy with Chinese character-istics, there have been rapid and substantial changes in the country's industrial management. One important policy is the importation of the "modern enterprise system" that, in practice, follows the modern Western-style and market-based corporate system. In addition to its critical role in the sustainable improvement of productivity in the industrial sector, industrial reform is also the institutional *sine qua non* in terms of establishing an effectively functioning competitive market system.

The reform on nonperforming SOEs was debated once more in the Fifth Plenum of the 14th CCPCC held during September 1995. The outcome was the policy of "grasping the large and releasing the small" (*zhua da fang xiao*). To "grasp the large" (*zhua da*) is to turn a select group of 300 out of a list of 1,000 already successful large enterprises and enterprise groups into world-class businesses. To "release the small" (*fang xiao*) is to privatize or to contract out small SOEs or to let them go bankrupt. This policy allows most small SOEs to be sold off to private individuals and the management of those not sold is contracted out. The majority of the remaining large and medium-sized SOEs were to be turned into corporations with various forms of ownership, ranging from corporations with 100 percent private ownership to those with a mixture of private and state capital, and others with 100 percent state capital. The central government, however, would continue to be the only shareholder in companies that produce "special-category" and defense-related products.

The state ownership, which had been defined as the classic feature of socialism, was discussed at the 15th CCP National Congress in October 1997. The CCP's final conclusion was that public (*gongyou*), instead of state (*guoyou*), ownership was to be the dominant form of ownership. (In the Chinese definition, state ownership only includes the SOEs, while public ownership includes both the SOEs and the COEs.) In addition, it encouraged the development of every other form of ownership, including private ownership. Furthermore, private and individual businesses were not only tolerated but also now considered to be making valuable contributions to the economy.

The shift in the CCP's view on ownership is now enshrined in the Chinese constitution with two amendments to the constitution at the Ninth National Congress of the NPC held in March 1998. The first amendment was to Article 6 of the constitution, which saw the addition of a clause stating that China is now at its preliminary stage of socialism. This amendment is used to justify having public, instead of state, ownership as the main form of ownership of the means of production. The clause further states that public ownership will develop alongside other forms of ownership. The second constitutional amendment was to Article 21, with the addition of a clause stating that individual, private, and other forms of nonpublic ownership are "important components of a socialist economy" and they "supplement the system of socialist public ownership."

FINANCE AND BANKING

To a large extent public finance determines the use of a nation's aggregate resources and, together with monetary and exchange rate policies, it influences the macro balance of payments, the accumulation of foreign debt, the rates of inflation, interest, and so on. However, the degree of impact may differ significantly and depend upon whether the economy is managed under the market-oriented system or under the centrally planned system. Public finance usually plays an important role in promoting balanced development and equilibrium in both wealth accumulation and distribution for a planned economy in which central government collects and directly dispenses much of its budget for society, while the local budget is collected from and used for local administrative organs, factories, enterprises, and welfare facilities. As the market economy is a private ownership system, the channels of policy influences are much more indirect and mainly through the laissez-faire approach.

Since the early 1980s, public finance, as an important component of the Chinese economic system, has undergone a series of reforms in terms of the development of central–local relations. The goals of these reforms were to decentralize the fiscal structure and to strengthen the incentive for local government to collect more revenue for themselves, and for the central government to maintain an egalitarian fiscal redistribution among the provinces. Briefly, China's efforts toward this end have experienced different stages, all of which sought to find a rational revenue-raising formula between the central and the local governments.

Since 1994, China has implemented a so-called "tax-sharing system" (*fenshui zhi*). At this stage, Chinese fiscal policy, through transferring much of the revenue collection function from local to central government, attempted to tackle the principal–agent problem of the revenue-contracting period. The solution was essentially to transpose the principal and agent. Under this system, China's tax revenues have been collected by and shared between central and local governments, as follows:

1. *Central taxes* (that is, those that are collected by the central government): these include customs duties; the operations tax paid by the railways, various banks and insurance companies; import-related VAT and consumption tax collected by the customs; consumption tax; and so on.
2. *Local taxes* (that is, those that are collected by local governments): these include operation tax (excluding the part paid by railway, various banks, and insurance companies); city and township land use tax; and so on.
3. *Shared taxes* (that is, those that are shared between central and local governments): these include domestic VAT (75 percent for central government); income tax (60 percent for central government); resource tax (except the tax paid by offshore oil enterprises, all the rest goes to local government); stamp tax in the stock market; and so on.

Since 1978, banking reforms have played an important role in China's overall efforts to transform a centrally planned economy into a market-based economy. Although the banking sector has undergone remarkable changes over the course of this period, deep-seated structural problems of asset quality, capital adequacy, and profitability continue to pose considerable challenges. In 1995, two notable developments in this respect were introduced: the promulgation of the Central Bank Law that firmly established the PBC as the sole government agent to supervise and regulate the banking sector; and the enactment of the Commercial Banking Law that clearly defined the scope of business for commercial banks.

The 1997 Asian financial crisis accelerated the pace of reform in China's banking system. China quickened the pace in 1998 and seems to be aware of two lessons that can be drawn from the Asian financial crisis. The first lesson is that a sound banking system is crucial for an economy to withstand external shocks. The second lesson from the Japanese banking saga is that delays will only allow nonperforming loans (NPLs) to grow and to erode the levels of bank capital. Under the reforms that began in December 1998, the directors of the regional branches of the PBC would be appointed directly by its headquarters in Beijing without consultations with the provincial governments. Instead of the previous arrangement of a PBC branch being established in each province and SEZ, the regional PBC branches were now located in only nine cities.[3] Furthermore, powers that had previously been delegated to PBC branches to control the volume of credit were concentrated in the central PBC headquarters. Moreover, projects above a certain scale would now have to be approved by central bank headquarters. However, only the above reform effort was not enough for the construction of a healthy banking and financing system, since there had been too many bad loans advanced to the SOEs (something that we will discuss in greater detail in the next section).

The reform of the SOEs was delayed as a result of the 1997 Asian financial crisis.[4] Two years later, in 1999, China introduced a debt–equity swap scheme (*zhai zhuan gu*), which would convert a portion of SOEs' bank debt into equity. China's four largest state-owned commercial banks set up their own state asset management companies—"Cinda" (of the China Construction Bank), "Huarong" (of the Industrial and Commercial Bank of China), "Great Wall" (of the Agricultural Bank of China), and "Oriental" (of the Bank of China)—to deal respectively with their bad loans to selected SOEs that have potential as going business concerns, but are burdened by heavy debts. The bad loans are converted into equity and then sold at a discount to investors. The immediate objectives of debt–equity swaps are to improve the balance sheet of the commercial banks and reduce the debt service of the SOEs. In the longer term, it is hoped that investors in these debt–equity swaps would have the managerial and technical expertise to turn the SOEs around permanently. There are strict guidelines specifying conditions that the first enterprises have to fulfill before they are allowed to have their debts converted into equity.

The conditions under which enterprises were chosen include: (1) they must have good marketing records and competitiveness; (2) their technical equipment must be in line with environmental protection; (3) they must have high-quality management and good accounting systems; (4) their leadership must be specialized in business and administration; and (5) they must take "effective reform measures," including plans to "cut the number of employees to increase efficiency." By the end of 1999, 601 nonperforming SOEs had been approved by the State Economic and Trade Commission (SETC) to transform their debts (459.6 billion yuan) into equity.

Since the late 1990s, several measures have been taken to establish a strong prudential framework that encompasses all types of banking and non-bank financial institutions. On April 1, 2000, China introduced a "real name" banking system under which all of the household bank deposits require a depositor's ID. This is an important step in moving from anonymous banking to real-name banking, an international practice. In reality, this change was concerned not so much with increasing tax revenue, as with reducing political corruption by making the flow of money transparent. A key issue in the recent economic development of China has been the value of its currency, especially in relation to the large trade surplus with the US. China has built up significant foreign reserves over recent years to support the value of the Renminbi (RMB). Until July 2005, the RMB was pegged to the dollar. In July 2005 a new system was announced under which the RMB is pegged against a basket of currencies and has now been allowed to fluctuate by 0.3 percent per day. At the same time, a revaluation of 2.1 percent against the US dollar was announced. Since revaluation, the RMB has appreciated by more than 20 percent against the US dollar.

China's access to the World Trade Organization (WTO) in 2001 has brought about major institutional improvements. These include: (1) liberalizing interest rates for bank deposits and bank loans, improving indirect policy tool, and abolishing directed, political lending; (2) continuing the commercialization process by allowing more competing and accepting diversified ownership structures, improving the quality of banks' assets through debt destructing and debt transfer, and increasing operational efficiency while reducing overstaffing and over-expansion; (3) continuing to develop securities markets by simplifying trading procedures, improving information disclosure procedures, and upgrading the legal framework; and (4) further simplifying the foreign exchange administration, allowing more exchange rate flexibility, starting a gradual removal of capital controls, and permitting foreign banks and other financial institutions to enter China, in accordance with the WTO agreement.

However, more reforms are still required. Specifically, China has yet to adopt a fully market-based monetary policy and policies of greater independent and accountability. In the coming years, a fully flexible exchange rate regime should be adopted, along with the gradual and cautious removal of capital control. And, if preconditions are met, full capital account convertibility should be adopted ultimately.

FUTURE PERSPECTIVE

While China's reform has been strongly driving its economic growth, it has also led to a series of socioeconomic problems. A glance at China's past social and economic transformations reveals that the large surge in income inequalities (see Chapter 6 for a detailed analysis) was not the only unwanted result of Chinese-style reform. The worsening of social and political progress during the 1990s and the 2000s is another example. For example, China's "control of corruption" score was more than 50 in 1996 (see Figure 5.3a), but it dropped to only 30 in 2007 (see Figure 5.3c); between 1996 and 2002 its score in terms of "voice and accountability" was among the lowest of all of the nations considered by the World Bank (see Figure 5.3b), and there is no sign of improvements between 2002 and 2007 (see Figure 5.3c). Without good reason, China's party–state political system has lacked the

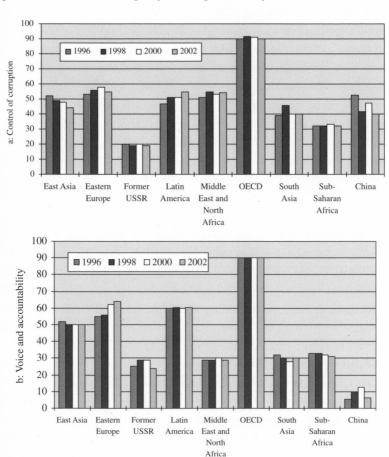

Note: The *y*-coordinates denote the degrees of "control of corruption" and "voice and accountability," respectively (100 = maximum level; 0 = minimum level).

Source: Created by the author, based on Kaufmann, D., Kraay, A. and Mastruzzi, M. "Governance Matters VII: Aggregate and Individual Governance Indicators, 1996–2007." *World Bank Policy Research Working Paper* No. 4654, Washington, D.C.: World Bank, 2008.

Figure 5.3   Social and political capacities, China and the world

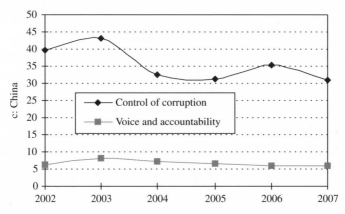

Figure 5.3   (continued)

informational and incentive roles of democracy that, working mainly through open public discussion, could be of pivotal importance for the reach of social and public policies.

Since the beginning of its economic reform policies, China has benefited increasingly from global interdependence and the modern world's free flow of goods, capital, and people. However, with those benefits have also come the responsibilities of accountability and transparency. China's party–state system has exposed the dearth of political dynamics. The Severe Acute Respiratory Syndrome (SARS) epidemic, which spread throughout China in April 2003, exposed some of China's institutional weakness.[5] Yet the greatest impact of the SARS crisis may be on China's antiquated political system. Chinese mismanagement of the outbreak plainly exposed just how far political reform has lagged behind economic development. Beijing's long concealment of the truth exposed political faultiness by simultaneously weakening the economy and damaging the government's credibility. The crisis has undermined traditional supporters, aggravating old demographic strains, and emboldening detractors to make more assertive protests against government policy. While the growing pressure from a more demanding public and an increasingly interdependent world has forced China to re-evaluate its political and socioeconomic policies, the extent of any resulting political reform depends upon whether or not the enhanced incentives for accountability and transparency among public officials override the traditional incentives for party and factional loyalty.

In short, for the majority of the past three decades, China's reform has achieved two objectives simultaneously: to improve economic efficiency by unleashing the standard forces of incentives and competition on the one hand; and on the other hand, to make the reform a win–win game and therefore in the interests of those in power (Qian 2007). They also take into consideration China's specific political and cultural conditions. With its impressive economic achievements, today the Chinese reform is rarely called into question. However, it still remained problematic in social and political perspectives throughout the reform era. Ironically, China's economic growth was obtained at the cost of thwarted political reforms, not to mention worsening income inequalities as well as other social problems. As China continues to integrate with the world economy and accepts other global values, there are mounting pressures for political reform.

Before ending our discussion on China's political economic transformations, let us finish our account of the story told by Hanfeizi at the beginning of this chapter:

> Feeling it strange, the Duke sent a man to ask Bianque for the reason. "Well, an ailment lying in between the skin and the muscles remains on the surface, and so external application with warm water and ointment can cure it," said Bianque. "If it sinks into muscles, acupuncture will do good; if it resides in the stomach and the intestines, a decoction of herbs will take effect. But when the sickness penetrates into the bone marrow, it becomes fatal and nothing can be done about it. Now, as the Duke has come to that last stage, I have nothing to recommend." Five days after that, the Duke felt pains and ordered his men to look for Bianque, but only to find that he had fled to the state of Qin. Soon afterward, the Duke died.

ENDNOTES

1   To be continued at the end of this chapter.

2   For example, the Tenth National People's Congress of March 2008 elected Hu Jintao as President with a total of 2,937 votes. Just four delegates voted against him, four abstained, and 38 did not vote.

3   They are Shanghai, Tianjin, Shenyang, Nanjing, Ji'nan, Wuhan, Guangzhou, Chengdu, and Xi'an, with additional two administrative departments housed in Beijing and Chongqing municipalities.

4   Before the crisis, there had been a call for the SOEs to be reconstructed according to the Korean model. But obviously this idea has been abandoned as soon as South Korea's *chaebols* met difficulties.

5   From November 2002 to 2003, SARS infected over 8,000 people in 30 countries and killed more than 500. In addition to the human toll, it was inflicting significant economic damage across Asia. Besides Hong Kong, which was among the worst hit, GDP growth rates in Taiwan, Singapore, and Thailand were also lower in 2003. Nowhere was SARS had more impact than on mainland China, where the disease started.

CHAPTER SIX

ECONOMIC GROWTH AND
SOCIAL JUSTICE

Bianzhong—traditional Chinese percussion instrument

Source: http://en.wikipedia.org
Note: Permission is granted to copy, distribute, and/or modify this document under the terms of the GNU Free
Documentation License, Version 1.3 or any later version published by the Free Software Foundation; with no Invariant
Sections, no Front-Cover Texts, and no Back-Cover Texts. A copy of the license is included in the section entitled "GNU Free
Documentation License."

China has experienced a period of rapid economic growth, accompanied by increased levels of income. While China's reform has been a
strong driver of its economic growth, it has also caused a series of
socioeconomic problems. Prior to the reform, China was an egalitarian
society in terms of income distribution. In the initial stage of the
reform, the policy of "letting some people get rich first" was adopted to

overcome egalitarianism in income distribution, to promote efficiency with strong incentives, and ultimately to realize common prosperity based on an enlarged pie. But this policy has quickly increased income gaps between different groups of people. In recent decades, China's income inequality has increased dramatically and the reduction of poverty is still posing considerable challenges to the social and economic harmony in China . . .

> To take the road to socialism is to realize common prosperity step by step. Our plan is as follows: where conditions permit, some areas may develop faster than others; those that develop faster can help promote the progress of those that lag behind, until all become prosperous. If the rich keep getting richer and the poor poorer, polarization will emerge. The socialist system must and can avoid polarization. One way is for the areas that become prosperous first to support the poor areas by paying more taxes or turning in more profits to the state. Of course, this should not be done too soon. At present, we don't want to dampen the vitality of the developed areas or encourage the practice of having everyone "eat from the same big pot." We should study when to raise this question and how to settle it.
> —Deng Xiaoping (1992, p. 374)

ECONOMIC GROWTH

Over the past few decades, the Chinese economy has experienced a number of dramatic changes. Specifically, China's macroeconomic performance experienced a steady growth in the first Five-Year Plan (1953–57), a short leap forward followed by a sudden economic disaster in the period 1958–62, a rapid growth period (1963–65), a chaotic period stemming from the "Cultural Revolution" movement (1966–76), and a fast growth period during the post-reform era with a few exceptions in 1981 and 1989–90 (see Figure 6.1). Particularly

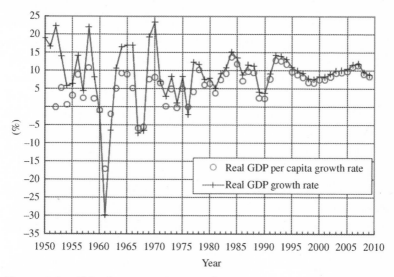

Figure 6.1 China's economic growth rates

praiseworthy in light of all of these developments is that the economic growth of China has sustained an average annual rate of about 10 percent since 1978, making it one of the most dynamic economies in the world during the same period. This average growth rate is approximately three times than the average of developed nations, more than double that of India, whose conditions are similar to those of China, and even higher than that of the newly industrialized economies (NIEs) including South Korea, Taiwan, Hong Kong, and Singapore.

China has already has the second largest GNP in the world, only behind the US. Although China's total GNP is large, its per capita GNP is lower than that of South Korea, Malaysia, and Thailand, but higher than that of other neighboring nations such as India, Mongolia, North Korea, and Vietnam. In addition, according to the standards of the World Bank, China has moved from a low-income economy to a middle-income economy by per capita GNP.[1] Using nominal exchange rates, in 2009 China's per capita GDP was less than one-tenth that of the US. However, nominal exchange rates underestimate the size of the Chinese economy because Chinese prices are much lower than those found in developed countries. If it is calculated by the purchasing power parity (PPP) rates, China's economic size would be much larger than it is as measured by the current exchange rate. Generally, even though they differ greatly, the per capita GDPs adjusted by PPP rates are between two and four times that measured by exchange rate.

While the PPP estimates are subject to some margin of error, the Chinese economy certainly has the potential to rival that of the US in size as a result of the enormous Chinese population. Arguably, the size of the Chinese economy may have been underestimated if international statistical standards are applied. For example, China's actual GDP could have been larger than the current figure, the gap of which is contributed by the following aspects: (1) real estate sector; (2) government, science and technology, education, culture, and health care sectors; (3) self-service within enterprises; (4) rural construction and other rural economic activities; and (5) national defense and underground economic activities.

The size of underground economic activities varies enormously from country to country. Obviously, it is impossible to get precise estimates because, by their very nature, the details have been largely hidden from the authorities, especially in transitional economies such as China. Nevertheless, the following factors could determine the size of the underground economy in China:

1. The level of taxes and regulations. The greater their level, the greater the incentive for people to evade the system and "go underground."
2. The determination of the authorities to catch up with evaders, and the severity of the punishments for those exposed.
3. The size of the service sector relative to the manufacturing sector. It is harder for the authorities to detect the illicit activities of motor mechanics, gardeners, and window cleaners than the output of cars, bricks, and soap.

4. The proportion of the population that is self-employed. It is much easier for the self-employed to evade taxes than it is for people receiving wages, where taxes are deducted at source.

It is generally admitted that the high rate of capital accumulation, or the high savings rate, has contributed to China's rapid economic growth. In China, investment is highly profitable because the surplus labor prevented the real wage from rising significantly, and the large pool of domestic savings prevented a rise in the interest rate. The importance of the latter is seen through household savings as a proportion of disposable income in China, which have been higher than those in most developed and developing nations. China's savings rate has been extremely high during the reform period. From 1978 to 1997, the average savings rate was 37.1 percent. By contrast, governmental savings kept falling in both absolute and relative terms. China's share of domestic savings was more than 50 percent in 1978, but fell below zero in the 1990s, showing a reversal from the circumstances of the command economy. From 1978 to 1988, the annual growth rate of private financial savings (including security assets) was more than 30 percent, and a similar increase occurred in the period 1989 to 1998 (Wu 2000). This rapid increase has been attributed to the following factors: expected uncertainty, income increase, deflation, nominal interest rates, the level of monetization in the economy, capital market development, and income inequality.

Another key factor behind China's impressive growth is its integration into the global economy. This is achieved through four channels. First, the access to international markets for labor-intensive manufactured goods accelerates the movement of labor out of low-productivity agriculture into high-productivity industry. Second, China is now able to buy modern technology (some of which was previously denied to China). Third, foreign direct investment (FDI) increases the level of capital stock, transfers new technology, makes available global distribution networks, and introduces domestic firms to more efficient management techniques. Fourth, the competition from international trade forces Chinese enterprises to be more efficient and innovative.

REGIONAL ECONOMIC DIFFERENCES

Natural and human resources are distributed unevenly in China. Specifically, the Eastern belt is blessed with a mild climate and rich soil, while the Western belt has a vast area and a sparse population. The northern part is much richer in mineral resources than the southern part, except for a few nonferrous metals. In contrast, most of the southern part, given its favorable climate and terrain, has an agricultural advantage over most of the northern part (especially the desert northwest region) and, in particular, dominates most of the nation's rice production. All of the above regional characteristics in the distribution of resources, together with the spatially diversified regional economic development policies that China has pursued in recent decades and other historical and cultural factors, have unevenly decided the spatial structure of the Chinese economy.

Since economic reform and open-door policies were implemented in the late 1970s, the Chinese economy has demonstrated an increasing asymmetry between different regions. This has resulted in a series of regional economic problems that need to be addressed properly by policymakers. Beginning with the common background of an ideological system and history, but proceeding with differing paces of economic reform and with different development policies, China has developed its provinces and promoted the welfare of urban and rural people differently. Not surprisingly, China's economic reform and open-door policies have over the past decades disproportionally aided the coastal provinces where per capita GDPs are several times higher than in the poorer inland provinces.

The provincial rankings, which are based on the estimated per capita GDP data for the selected years (1952, 1979, 1990, and 2000), are shown in Table 6.1. In 1952, the per capita national income of Shanghai was estimated at 584.15 yuan, which is 10.67 times that of Guizhou (54.77 yuan). In 1979, Shanghai's per capita national income, at constant prices, had risen to 2,860.92 yuan, 27.85 times the figure for Guizhou (102.72 yuan). Obviously, during the pre-reform period, there was a rapid widening of the economic gap between the richest and poorest provinces.

How large is this gap during the post-reform period? If we consider per capita GDP the economic gap has experienced two different patterns. Shanghai's per capita GDP was 27.88 times that of Guizhou's in 1979 and 7.34 times that of Guizhou's in 1990. This implies that the per capita GDP ratio of Shanghai to Guizhou decreased greatly during the above period. From 1990 onward, however, the per capita GDP ratio of Shanghai to Guizhou was exceeded once again by 12. China's per capita GDP ratio of more than 12 for the richest (Shanghai) to the poorest (Guizhou) is only lower than that of Indonesia (20.8, 1983), but much higher than those of many other countries, such as the former Yugoslavia (7.8, 1988), India (3.26, 1980), the Netherlands (2.69, 1988), Italy (2.34, 1988), Canada (2.30, 1988), Spain (2.23, 1988), France (2.15, 1988), West Germany (1.93, 1988), Greece (1.63, 1988), the UK (1.63), South Korea (1.53, 1985), Japan (1.47, 1981), the US (1.43, 1983), and Australia (1.13, 1978).[2]

Table 6.1 Provincial Ranks by Per Capita GDP, Selected Years

Province	1952[a]	1980	1990	2000
Anhui	22	27	24	24
Beijing	3	2	2	2
Chongqing	NP	NP	NP	19
Fujian	14	20	12	7
Gansu	16	16	27	30
Guangdong	18	18	5	5
Guangxi	27	28	29	29
Guizhou	29	29	30	31
Hainan	NP	NP	15	15
Hebei	9	7	17	11
Heilongjiang	4	5	8	10
Henan	23	21	28	18
Hubei	20	17	13	13
Hunan	21	22	20	17
Inner Mongolia	7	14	18	16
Jiangsu	13	10	7	6

(continued)

Table 6.1 (Continued)

Province	1952[a]	1980	1990	2000
Jiangxi	11	24	23	25
Jilin	8	6	10	14
Liaoning	5	4[a]	4	8
Ningxia	10	19	19	22
Qinghai	15	9	14	20
Shaanxi	24	12	. 21	27
Shandong	19	13	11	9
Shanghai	1	1	1	1
Shanxi	17	15	16	21
Sichuan	28	26	26	23
Tianjin	2	3	3	3
Tibet	25[b]	23[b]	22	26
Xinjiang	6	11	9	12
Yunnan	26	25	25	28
Zhejiang	12	8	6	4

Notes
1 Per capita GDP data are measured at current prices.
2 "NP" denotes "not a province for the year."
[a] Per capita GDP is estimated based on the data of national income (SSB various years (1990)).
[b] Per capita GDP is estimated by the author based on the Tibet/Yunnan ratio of national incomes (1.127) and Yunnan's GDP data.
Source: Guo, R. *How the Chinese Economy Works.* 3rd ed. London and New York: Palgrave-Macmillan, 2009a.

China's regional economic differences have existed over a long period of its history. In addition, resulting from the diversified natural and social conditions among the country's different regions, its purchasing powers have also differed from region to region. For example, the following information reflects a large degree of inter-regional differences for the retail prices of some foodstuffs (as of September 2009):[3]

- 1 kg of chicken costs ¥12.06 in Jiangxi, but ¥32.00 in Shanghai;
- 1 kg of fish costs ¥10.04 in Jiangxi, but ¥20.10 in Tibet;

- 1 kg of pork costs ¥21.76 in Xinjiang, but ¥32.00 in Beijing;
- 1 kg of eggs costs ¥6.8 in Shanghai, but ¥10.96 in Hainan;
- 1 kg of milk costs only ¥3.78 in Xinjiang, but ¥17.4 in Shanghai;
- 1 kg of apples costs only ¥4.12 in Henan, but ¥13.16 in Chongqing;
- 1 kg of oranges costs only ¥3.04 in Henan, but ¥7.00 in Qinghai and Tibet;
- 1 kg of bananas costs only ¥2.98 in Jiangxi, but ¥7.00 in Chongqing.

Although commercial activities are subject to a uniform regulatory system set by the central government, provincial and local officials have a large degree of discretion in terms of the enforcement of national legislation. In recent years, the World Bank, in collaboration with the Chinese Academy of Social Sciences, has conducted a series of annual assessments on the ease of doing business in China. These studies found that the investment climate varies widely across provinces, even though the laws and regulations are fundamentally the same throughout the country. As measured by the four indicators (starting a business, registering property, getting credit and registering collateral, and enforcing contracts) in Table 6.2, the coastal provinces (such as Guangdong, Jiangsu, Shanghai, Zhejiang, Shandong, and Fujian) have the most favourable environments for conducting business. The western and central provinces, however, seem to have the most challenging business environments. Nevertheless, most provinces measured have at least one indicator that compares favourably with other surveyed provinces.

Before the reform, there was a rather uneven distribution of income between rural and urban areas. In 1957 when the Chinese economy was at its most prosperous, the per capita personal income in urban areas was 3.48 times that found in rural areas (SSB various years (1986, pp. 667 and 673)). As shown in Figure 6.2, the income gap between the rural and urban areas continued to decrease until 1983, but after 1985 the gap began to widen again and by 1994 the rural–urban

Table 6.2 Ease of Doing Business in China—Top and Bottom 10 Provinces

Rank No.	Starting a Business	Registering Property	Getting Credit	Enforcing Contracts
1	Zhejiang	Shanghai	Fujian	Guangdong
2	Jiangsu	Guangdong	Jiangsu	Jiangsu
3	Guangdong	Fujian	Guangdong	Zhejiang
4	Shandong	Shandong	Shandong	Shanghai
5	Shanghai	Jiangsu	Shanghai	Shaanxi
6	Beijing	Tianjin	Tianjin	Shandong
7	Fujian	Zhejiang	Beijing	Tianjin
8	Tianjin	Jilin	Zhejiang	Chongqing
9	Liaoning	Chongqing	Hebei	Beijing
10	Jilin	Shaanxi	Heilongjiang	Liaoning
. . .	. . .	. . .	. . .	. . .
21	Jiangxi	Hebei	Jilin	Heilongjiang
22	Hunan	Yunnan	Qinghai	Xinjiang
23	Qinghai	Hainan	Yunnan	Sichuan
23	Yunnan	Hunan	Jiangxi	Guizhou
25	Shaanxi	Hubei	Guizhou	Jilin
26	Ningxia	Shanxi	Xinjiang	Anhui
27	Anhui	Henan	Ningxia	Hunan
28	Guangxi	Guizhou	Shaanxi	Qinghai
29	Gansu	Gansu	Gansu	Yunnan
30	Guizhou	Guangxi	Guangxi	Gansu

Notes
1 Each province is represented by its capital city.
2 Hong Kong, Macau, Taiwan, and Tibet are excluded.
Source: World Bank. *Doing Business in China 2008*. Beijing: Social Sciences Literature Press, 2008, pp. 38–9.

inequalities were even greater than during the mid-1960s and 1970s. Since the reform, the income differentials between urban and rural China have experienced different patterns. In the early period of the economic reform, which was focused on the introduction of the

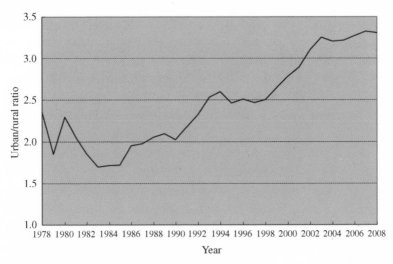

Figure 6.2 China's rural–urban income gaps

household responsibility system (HRS) to the agricultural sector, the level of rural income increased very rapidly and the gap between the rural and urban areas narrowed until 1985. Since then, the rural–urban gap has begun to increase again as a result of the diminishing marginal returns of the agricultural sector on the one hand and robust urban growth spurred by industrial reforms on the other. As demonstrated in Figure 6.2, the ratio of urban to rural per capita income fell from 2.36 in 1978 to 1.70 in 1983; it has been in excess of 3.0 since 2000.[4]

From the late 1970s, China has adopted an uneven spatial development strategy, encouraging a portion of regions to go one step further to get rich. This included differing development preferences among different regions and during different periods. To date, the most successful regional development strategy is the so-called "Coastal Area Development Strategy." This strategy, which will be mentioned in Chapter 7, has benefited significantly from China's open-door policy. The final, major outcome of this strategy, a fact well known to us, has been the dramatic growth of foreign direct investment and foreign trade, which have been substantial drivers of the Chinese

economy—and of the coastal area in particular. The additional outcome of this strategy is the increasing economic disparity between
China's coastal and western areas in recent decades.

After 20 years of development, in 1999, the Chinese government
started to talk publicly about the introduction of changes to China's
regional development policy. One challenge facing China in the era of
globalization was to prevent its uneven growth pattern. In order
to narrow the gap with the prosperous coastal area, the CCPCC
propagated a campaign called the "Western Region Development
Strategy" (*xibu da kaifa*), which constitutes a cornerstone of the tenth
Five-Year Plan (2001–2005) and is intended to foster the future
development of the inland regions. The stated goals were to bring
about social and economic development of the interior and western
regions of China. In November 1999, the State Council appointed the
newly formed "State Council Leading Group for Western Region
Development" to define a new policy. The "Office" was established in
January 2003 to deal with day-to-day business. It was anticipated that
the strategy would initiate a number of programs and projects to
stimulate domestic demand, expand the market, and maintain sustained, rapid, and healthy development of the national economy.

The Northeast region includes the three provinces of Jilin,
Heilongjiang, and Liaoning. Formerly called Manchuria, this region
had been relatively more industrialized than other Chinese regions at
the beginning of the People's Republic. The main reasons for this are
twofold: much of its industrial capacity was preserved after the
Japanese were defeated at the end of World War II; and China's
close ties with the former USSR during the 1950s had placed most of
their cooperative, industrial projects within the Northeast region.
During the early 1960s and 1970s, as a result of worsening relations
with the former USSR, the Northeast region had become a border
area facing the high probability of war that China had to prepare for
against the USSR. Since the 1980s, the Northeast region has lagged
behind other regions (especially the southeast and coastal provinces).
In 2002 a new spatial initiative entitled the "Resurgence of the Old

Industrial Base in the Northeast Region" was announced. As suggested by the name of the policy, its purpose was to address the increasing obsolescence of the industrial base of the Northeast region. In order to implement a regional coordinated development during the entire tenth Five-Year Plan (2000–2005), the State Council spent 100 billion yuan in the Northeast region as part of its proposal to upgrade industries and to provide greater incentives for modernization.

HOW (UN)EQUAL IS THE CHINESE SOCIETY?

As noted above, while China's reform has been a strong driver of its economic growth, it has also derived a series of socioeconomic problems. Prior to the reform, China was an egalitarian society in terms of income distri-bution. In the initial stage of the reform, the policy of "letting some people get rich first" (*rang yi bufen ren xian fu qilai*) was adopted in order to overcome egalitarianism in income distribution, to promote efficiency with strong incentives, and to ultimately realize common prosperity based on an enlarged pie. But this policy has quickly enlarged income gaps between different groups of people.

Economic inequality has several dimensions. Economists are mostly concerned with the income and consumption dimensions. Non-income inequality includes inequality in skills, education, opportunities, happiness, health, wealth, and other similar factors. Although other approaches are also useful in economic analysis, the Gini coefficient has been most frequently applied by economists worldwide to measure the level of income inequality. Developed by the Italian statistician Corado Gini in 1912, the Gini coefficient is most prominently used as a measure of inequality of income distribution or inequality of wealth distribution. It is defined as a ratio with values between 0 and 1: a low Gini coefficient indicates more equal income or wealth distribution, while a high Gini coefficient implies a more unequal pattern of distribution. In extreme cases, 0 corresponds to perfect equality (when everyone has exactly the same income) and 1

Table 6.3 China's Income Gini Coefficients, Selected Years

Year	Rural Area	Urban Area	China as a Whole
1952	0.230	0.165	0.255
1979/80	0.310	0.160	0.330
1988	0.338	0.233	0.382
1995	0.381	0.280	0.437
2002	0.366	0.319	0.454
2007	0.370	0.399	0.496

Sources
1 World Bank. *China: The Development of a Socialist Economy.* Washington DC: World Bank, 1983, pp. 83 and 92, for 1979/80.
2 Zhao, R. 'Increasing Income Inequality and Its Causes in China.' In: C. Riskin, R. Zhao, and Li Shi (eds), *China's Retreat from Equality: Income Distribution and Economic Transition.* New York: M.E. Sharpe, 2001, pp. 25–43, for 1988 and 1995.
3 Li, S. 'China's Urban and Rural Income Surveys.' *Journal of Financial Economics* (in Chinese), 2004, no. 3 for 2002.
4 www.ahpc.gov.cn for 2007.

corresponds to perfect inequality (when one person has all the income, while all remaining people have zero income).

Compared with other countries, China's Gini coefficients (see Table 6.3) have been very high, only lower than those of a few nations in Latin America and Africa, whereas the latter have been usually regarded as the most unequal economies in the world. Nevertheless, there have been two different views with respect to the current situation of income inequality in China. One view supposes that China's Gini coefficients have been underestimated since in most, if not all cases the earnings of the low-income groups were usually overestimated, whereas those of the higher income groups were usually underestimated. For example, in some poor agricultural households a portion of earnings had to be used for productive investment and, as a result, the earnings that can be used for consumption will be reduced. By contrast, in the urban, high-income group some earnings and welfare payments were not included in the current reckoning of incomes (Ge 2000). However, there is a different view with respect to this issue: China's current income inequality has been overestimated and, if measured in terms of purchasing power parity (PPP) rates, China's income inequality should have been reduced considerably. In most cases, the price levels in poor areas are much lower than those in rich areas.

China has experienced rapid economic growth with a major impact on inequality in recent decades. Based on the survey data, Riskin et al. (2001) provide a comprehensive analysis of inequality and poverty in China for the years 1988 and 1995; and Gustafsson et al. (2008) extend this analysis through to the year 2002. They observe major changes in the composition of income between the two survey dates. Rural household income, mainly from farming, has declined from 74 percent to 56 percent, while non-farming wages increased from 9 percent to 22 percent, resulting in increasing levels of income inequality. The Gini ratio for rural income grew by 23 percent from 0.34 to 0.42 due to the unequal distribution of faster growing wage components of rural income. The corresponding increases in inequality in the urban areas were 43 percent in seven years from 0.23 to 0.33. The increasing inequality of distribution of income caused a rise in the level of urban income inequality. The wage share of income grew from 44 percent to 61 percent. Other components of income such as that of retirees and housing rental were subject to fast growth as well. Subsidies declined from 20 percent of urban income to 1 percent.

A substantial literature has analyzed the effects of income inequalities on macroeconomic performances, as reflected in rates of economic growth. Most argue that greater income inequality is an impediment to economic growth. A seemingly plausible argument points to the existence of credit market failures such that people are unable to exploit growth-promoting opportunities for investment. With only limited access to credit, investment opportunities depend upon individuals' levels of assets and incomes. Specifically, poor households tend to forego human capital investments that offer relatively high rates of return. In this case, a distortion-free redistribution of assets and incomes from rich to poor tends to raise the quantity and average productivity of investment. With declining marginal products of capital, the output loss from the market failure will be greater for the poor. So the higher the proportion of poor people there are in the economy, the lower the rate of growth.

A second way in which inequality could affect the future levels of economic growth is through political channels. The degree of inequality could affect the median voter's desired pattern of policies or it could determine individuals' ability to access political markets and participate in costly lobbying. If the mean income in an economy exceeds the median income, then a system of majority voting tends to favor the redistribution of resources from the rich to the poor. As the median voter's distance from the average capital endowment in the economy increases with the aggregate inequality of wealth, he or she will be led to approve a higher tax rate. This in turn could reduce incentives for productive investment, resulting in lower levels of growth. If this is correct, democratic societies with a more unequal distribution of wealth should be characterized by the exploitation of the rich by the poor—that is, high taxes and, consequently, low investment and growth, whereas undemocratic ones with similar characteristics would not.

Indeed, the negative effects of income inequality might exist in almost every sphere of human life. But there also exists some evidence that supports the view that income inequality could encourage economic growth—both directly and indirectly. The most intuitive thesis is that a lower degree of inequality would mean a greater amount of redistribution from the rich to the poor. It is this redistribution that would become an impediment to the creation of incentives for people (especially the poorest and richest groups of them) to work hard. There is also a positive view for the effect of inequality on economic growth: if individual savings rates rise with the level of income, then a redistribution of resources from the rich to the poor tends to lower the aggregate rate of savings in an economy. Through this channel, a rise in income inequality tends to raise the level of investment. In this case, greater inequality would enhance economic growth. However, there is an argument that inequality may lead to higher fertility rates, which could, in turn, reduce economic growth.

POVERTY AND SOCIAL SECURITY

With regard to the term "poverty," there have been two separate definitions—"broad poverty" and "deep poverty." Specifically, the first refers to the threshold that is based on the cost of 2,100 kilocalories per person per day with an adjustment for non-food purchases, broadly consistent with the preference of low-income consumers; the second relates to the threshold, which is defined as 80 percent of the broad poverty threshold.

China experienced rapid economic growth after economic reform, accompanied by increased income levels. However, a reduction in poverty is still a formidable task in China. Until the mid-1980s, the total number of poor had been reduced; since then, however, this has grown continuously, especially in urban areas. From 1988 to 1995, for example, the incidence of "broad poverty" in the urban area fell by a percentage of 0.2 percent—from 8.2 percent to 8.0 percent of the total urban population. Moreover, the urban population itself grew rapidly. As a result, the total number of urban broad poor rose by 19.6 percent during the period; that is, from 23.5 million people in 1988 to 28.1 million people in 1995 (Khan and Riskin 2001, p. 128).

This situation persists into the early twenty-first century and some scholars have put the total number of China's urban poor as even larger. According to a report undertaken by the Asian Development Bank (2002), China's urban poverty has varied considerably from province to province. Specifically, China's provinces can be classified into five groups by the incidences of "broad poverty" (that is, <2 percent, 2–4 percent, 4–6 percent, 6–8 percent, and >8 percent):

1. <2 percent (including Beijing, Jiangsu, Zhejiang, and Guangdong);

2. 2–4 percent (including Shanghai, Fujian, Hunan, Guangxi, Yunnan, Anhui, and Jiangxi);
3. 4–6 percent (including Hebei, Hubei, Guizhou, Chongqing, Qinghai, Shandong, and Sichuan);
4. 6–8 percent (including Tianjin, Inner Mongolia, Liaoning, Jillin, Hainan, Xinjiang, Shanxi, Heilongjiang, and Gansu);
5. >8 percent (including Henan, Shaanxi, Ningxia, and Tibet).

A simulation exercise conducted by Khan and Riskin (2001, p. 127) shows that by 1995 this high level of income growth in the urban area would have reduced the broad poverty rate to under 1 percent of the urban population, had the distribution of urban income remained unchanged between 1988 and 1995. In other words, had there been no rise in inequality, such a rapid increase in average incomes would have sufficed virtually to eradicate urban poverty. This rise in inequality, however, offset the rise in per capita income and, as a result, the estimated effect on the incidence of poverty ranges from an insignificant improvement to a significant deterioration, depending on the poverty indicator used and the cost of living index chosen to adjust the poverty income threshold.

Before reform, China's social security system had been a "pay-as-you-go" system, in which the funding to the older generation had to come from the contributions of the young generation. This kind of social security system has some defects. For example, since China's first implementation of a strict family planning policy in the early 1980s, most families, especially those in the urban areas, have had only one child, and the burden of supporting the old generation under a "pay-as-you-go" system was high and placed an unfair burden on the younger generation. According to the "Decision on Issues Concerning the Establishment of a Socialist Market Economic Structure," which was adopted by the Third Plenum of the Fourteenth National Party Congress in November 1993, the aim of the reform of the social security system was to establish the criterion of efficiency as the first priority, while considering fairness at the same time, and to change the "pay-as-you-go" system to a funding system that is based upon the contribution of the recipients themselves. In addition, the collection and payment of social security funding will be unified. In September 1997, the State Council promulgated a document relating to the safeguarding of minimum living standards for urban inhabitants in China.

Currently, pension insurance covers, in principle, all state-owned and other ownership enterprises in urban areas and also some non-public-owned enterprises and rural areas. The challenge of this reform comes from the funding of the pensions of older workers, who had received relatively low salaries during the course of their working lives. A large proportion of their salary was channeled into investment and construction while they were promised pensions after they retired. Following the implementation of the funding system, their pension will come from the selling of some state-owned enterprises or assets. The medical care system consists of four parts: compulsory basic medical insurance, supplementary medical insurance freely chosen by enterprises, commercial medical insurance freely chosen by individuals and social medical rescuing system. The principle of compulsory basic medical insurance is "low level, wide coverage." The criterion of minimum living standards and the entailing fund are the tasks of local governments. However, the majority of people, rural inhabitants, still face a weak, if any, social security system. They have to rely on their own deposits or the support of their relatives and offspring.

ENDNOTES

1   The World Bank (1996, pp. 394–5) defined low-income economies, lower middle-income economies, upper middle-income economies, and high-income economies with per capita GNPs of US$725 or less, US$726–2,895, US$2,896–8,955, and US$8,956 or more, respectively.

2   Data sources: Ottolenghi and Steinherr (1993, p. 29), Savoie (1992, p. 191), Smith (1987, p. 41), Higgins (1981, pp. 69–70), Nair (1985, p. 9), Hill and Weidemann (1989, pp. 6–7), Kim and Mills (1990, p. 415), and Hu et al. (1995, p. 92).

3   Source: China Price Information Network (www.chinaprice.gov.cn).

4   The understatement of income sources may miscalculate the income gap between the two. If taking into account the subsidies and other earnings in kind, the actual urban-to-rural ratio of incomes would have been as high as 5–6 times during the early 2000s (Li 2004), which was the largest in the world.

CHAPTER SEVEN

INTERNATIONAL ECONOMIC ENGAGEMENT

The travels of Zhang Qian to the West, Mogao cave no. 323, Dunhuang, Gansu

Source: http://en.wikipedia.org
Note: This image is in the public domain because its copyright has expired. This applies to the United States, Australia, the European Union, and those countries with a copyright term of life of the author plus 70 years.

The Silk Road (Silu) is the most well-known trading route in ancient China. Trade in silk grew under the Han dynasty (202 BC–AD 220), during which the Chinese traded silk for medicines, perfumes, and slaves in addition to precious stones. The Silk Road was an important path for cultural, commercial, and technological exchange between traders, merchants, pilgrims, missionaries, soldiers, nomads, and urban dwellers from different parts of the world. Trade on the Silk Road was a significant factor in the development of the great civilizations of India, China, Egypt, Persia, Arabia, and Rome, and in several respects helped lay the foundations for the modern world. During the Tang dynasty, trade along the Silk Road had declined. It revived tremendously during the eleventh and twelfth centuries when China became largely dependent on its silk trade. In addition, trade to Central and Western Asia as well as Europe recovered for a period from 1276–1368 under the Yuan dynasty when the Mongols controlled China. As overland trade became increasingly dangerous, and overseas trade became more popular, trade along the Silk Road declined . . .

> A man of the state of Lu (in today's southern Shandong province) was skilled in weaving hemp sandals and his wife was good at weaving fine white silk. The couple was thinking of moving out to the state of Yue (in today's Zhejiang province). "You will be in dire straits," he was told. "Why?" asked the man of the Lu. "Hemp sandals are for walking but people of the Yue walk barefoot. White silk is for making hats but people of the Yue go about bareheaded. If you go to a place where your skills are utterly useless, how can you hope to do well?"
> —*Hanfeizi* (280–233 BC)

HISTORICAL BACKGROUND

China had been a typical autarkic society for a long time before it was forced to open up to the outside world at the end of the First Opium War (1840–42). In the later period of the Qing dynasty (AD 1644–1911), *haijin* (ban on maritime voyages) included:

1. the export of cereals and five metals (gold, silver, copper, iron, and tin) were strictly prohibited;

2. private trade and contacts between Chinese and foreign businessmen were illegal;
3. foreigners' activities in China were only allowed on condition that "At most 10 foreigners may take a walk together near their hotel on the 8th, 18th and 28th days a month," "Overseas businessmen should not stay in Guangdong in winter," "Women from foreign countries are prohibited to enter this country," and so on;
4. Chinese businessmen going abroad were subject to the conditions that "At most one liter of rice may be carried by a seaman a day" and "At most two guns may be installed in a ship";
5. the manufacture of seagoing vessels of more than 500 *dan* (hectoliters) in weight and eight meters in height was prohibited.[1]

Western influence in China came about at the beginning of the fifteenth and sixteenth centuries due to the increased trade in Chinese products, such as silk and tea through the Silk Road that stretched from northwestern China to eastern Europe. The Europeans were interested in Hong Kong's safe harbor located on the trade routes of the Far East, thus establishing a trade enterprise between Western businessmen and China. The Portuguese were the first to reach China in 1555, but the British dominated foreign trade in the southern region of Guangdong during the early stages of Western connection in China. Ships from the British East India Company were stationed on the Indian Coast after Emperor Kangxi (reign 1654–1722) of the Qing dynasty (1644–1911) opened trade on a limited basis in Guangzhou. Fifteen years later, the company was allowed to build a storage warehouse outside Guangzhou. The Westerners were given limited preferences and had to adhere to many Chinese rules and policies. In addition, Chinese rulers also banned foreigners from learning the Chinese language in fear of their potential bad influences.

Chinese commodities, principally porcelain, were popular among European aristocrats. However, the levels of European imports from China were far greater than its exports. As a result, the British East

India Company tried to equalize its huge purchases from China by doubling its sales of opium to China. The sale of opium saw a great increase by the turn of the nineteenth century. Fearful of the outflow of silver, the Chinese emperor banned the drug trade in 1799, but to no avail. Following the end of the first Opium War, the Treaty of Nanjing in 1842 ceded Hong Kong to Britain in perpetuity. With the involvement of the British, many companies transferred from Guangzhou to Hong Kong, enabling the British colony to begin a prime Asian entrepôt. Hostilities between the British and the Chinese of China continued to heighten, leading to the Second Opium War. In 1860, the "Convention of Peking" ensured that Britain gained Kowloon, Stonecutters Island, and some other small islands.

From the middle of the nineteenth century, the Chinese economy had been transformed as a result of the gradual destruction of the feudal system. There was a gradual flow of foreign capital into the mainland, which was followed by the penetration of Western culture, which saw the first stirrings of Chinese industrialization. Unfortunately, because of long civil wars, as well as the invasion by the Japanese, China's economic development had not been given a high priority during the first half of the twentieth century. During the period of the first Five-Year Plan (1953–57), some economic progress was achieved. Thereafter, however, difficulties took place due to China's frequent domestic political struggles and the "closed-door" policies toward both the US-dominated capitalist bloc and the USSR-dominated socialist bloc.

As soon as the PRC was founded on October 1, 1949, the Chinese government severed almost all economic ties with the capitalist world. Affected by the Korean War (1950–53) and the Taiwan Strait crisis, the Eastern belt stagnated. However, it should be noted that China's foreign trade with the centrally planned economies (CPEs) usually remained at a minimum level, aiming at just supplementing any gap between domestic supply and demand. Such trade reflected natural resource endowments more than anything else. Therefore, China's close ties with the socialist economies did not result in significant economic effects on the Western belt. During the period from the early 1960s to the late 1970s, China practiced autarkic socialism as a result of the Sino–USSR disputes, as well as the implementation of the "self-reliance and independence" strategy thereafter.

For thousands of years, Chinese culture attempted to achieve a harmonious balance between Confucianism, Buddhism, and Taoism, which worked quite well for a very long time. Probably as a result, the Chinese were too intoxicated with past prosperity and still had proudly considered themselves at the "center of the world," even when it was clear that in economic terms China had lagged well behind Western nations. This kind of ethnocentrism and self-satisfaction meant that China remained a typical autarkic society. With regard to the cultural differences between the Chinese and Japanese economies, Maddison (1996, p. 53) states:

> In China, the foreigners appeared on the fringes of a huge country. The ruling elite regarded it as the locus of civilization, and considered the "barbarian" intruders an irritating nuisance. In Japan, they struck in the biggest city, humiliated the Shogun and destroyed his legitimacy as a ruler. The Japanese had already borrowed important elements of Chinese civilization and saw no shame in copying a Western model which had demonstrated its superior technology so dramatically.

CHINA OPENS ITS DOOR

For a long period after the founding of the PRC in 1949, the Chinese economy was a closed economy. China's external economic strategy began to experience dramatic changes in the late 1970s when the top Chinese policymakers suddenly found that the economy, having been constructed along socialist lines for almost 30 years, had lagged far behind not only the Western nations but also those once backward economies along the western coast of the Pacific Ocean.

In order to attract foreign investment, China enacted, in 1979, the "Law of the People's Republic of China Concerning the Joint Ventures with Chinese and Foreign Investment." Also, the CCPCC and State Council decided to grant Guangdong and Fujian provinces "special policies and flexible measures" in foreign economic affairs. On December 26, 1979, the People's Congress of Guangdong province approved the proposal of the provincial government that a part of Shenzhen next to Hong Kong, Zhuhai next to Macau, and Santou should all be permitted to experiment with a market-oriented economy with Chinese characteristics; namely, special economic zones (SEZs). This proposal was finally accepted by the NPC on August 26, 1980. At the same time, Xiamen in the southeast Fujian province, with its close proximity to Taiwan, also became a SEZ with the approval of the NPC.

Subsequently, Guangdong and Fujian gained substantial autonomy in developing their regions as the central government granted them authority to pursue reform "one step ahead" (*xian zhou yibu*). As a result, not only did these areas enjoy lower tax rates, but they also gained more authority over economic development. The four cities are below the provincial level, but have independent budget agreements with the central government; they have the authority to approve foreign investment projects of up to US$30 million, while other regions' authority remained much less.

Thereafter, a series of open-door measures were implemented in the coastal area: in October 1983, Hainan Island, Guangdong province, was allowed to conduct some of the special foreign economic policies granted to the SEZs; in April 1984, 14 coastal cities (Tianjin, Shanghai, Dalian, Qinhuangdao, Yantai, Qingdao, Lianyungang, Nantong, Ningbo, Wenzhou, Fuzhou, Guangzhou, Ganjiang, and Beihai) were designated by the CCPCC and the State Council as "open cities;" in February 1985, the three deltas of the Yangtze River, the Pearl River and South Fujian were approved as coastal economic development zones (EDZs); in March 1988, the expansion of the EDZs of all three deltas was again approved while at the same time some cities and counties in Liaodong and Shandong peninsulas and Bohai Basin area were allowed to open up economically to the outside world; in April 1988, the NPC approved the establishment of Hainan province, which was organized as a SEZ with even more flexible policies than other SEZs; in April 1990, Shanghai's suggestion to speed up the development of the Pudong area using some of the SEZ's mechanisms was approved by the CCPCC and the State Council.

In addition to its 14,500 km coastline, China has more than 22,000 km of international land boundaries. Specifically, nine provinces are directly exposed to the outside world. These frontier provinces, the neighboring nations, and the lengths of their respective borderlines are as detailed below:

- Gansu (with Mongolia, 65 km);
- Guangxi (with Vietnam, 1,020 km);
- Heilongjiang (with Russia, 3,045 km);
- Inner Mongolia (with Mongolia, 3,640 km; and Russia, 560 km);
- Jilin (with North Korea, 870 km; and Russia, 560 km);
- Liaoning (with North Korea, 546 km);
- Tibet (with India, 1,906 km; Nepal, 1,236 km; Bhutan, 470 km; and Myanmar, 188 km);
- Xinjiang (with Russia, 40 km; Mongolia, 968 km; Pakistan, 523 km; Kazakhstan, 1,533 km; Kyrgyzstan, 858 km; Tajikistan, 540 km; Afghanistan, 76 km; and India, 1,474 km);
- Yunnan (with Myanmar, 1,997 km; Laos, 710 km; and Vietnam, 1,353 km).

Generally, cross-border economic cooperation and trade are facilitated by both geographical factors and also the fact that people on both sides of the border often belong to the same minority group and share many cultural characteristics. China's border development has mainly benefited from its "open-door" policy and *rapprochement* with the neighboring countries since the mid-1980s. In 1984 the Chinese government promulgated the "Provisional Regulations for the Management of 'Small-volume' Border Trade" and opened up hundreds of frontier cities and towns. In contrast to the eastern coastal development, which was fueled principally by foreign direct investment

(FDI), China's inland frontier development has been characterized by border trade with its foreign neighbors. Since the early 1990s, a series of favorable and flexible measures to manage cross-border trade and economic cooperation have been granted to those frontier provinces.

Prior to the early 1980s, the management of foreign economic affairs rested in the hand of one government ministry that maintained an overly rigid control of matters. In the first years of the implementation of China's outward-oriented development strategy, the reform of the foreign economic system was conducted via three aspects. First, under the unified control of the state, there was a closer relationship between production and marketing, and between industry and trade, which enabled production units to participate directly in foreign trade. Second, the special policies and measures relating to foreign trade were handed to the local governments. A third type of reform was to expand the autonomy of the state-owned enterprises (SOEs) to act on their own initiatives and have direct links with foreign traders at meetings arranged by specialized export SOEs.

In 1982, the Ministry of Foreign Trade (MFT) was renamed the Ministry of Foreign Economic Relations and Trade (MFERT). At the same time, trade bureaus were established at the provincial and local levels to manage both foreign trade and FDI. The MFERT and local trade bureaus were, in principle, not allowed to interfere in the management of foreign trade enterprises. Many large SOEs received permission to engage in foreign trade. Local enterprises were also able to establish their own foreign trade companies. In 1988, foreign trade was reformed by a system of contracts under which the separation between ownership (state) and management (enterprise) was maintained and thus foreign trade enterprises were able to operate independently. Despite these reforms, the fundamental structure of central planning and state ownership has not been changed fundamentally, particularly in large and medium-sized SOEs.

Before the 1980s, international trade was in the hands of central government planning, which controlled more than 90 percent of trade by monopolizing the imports and exports of more than 3,000 kinds of commodities. These commodities can be classified into two categories: plan-commanded goods (in which both the value and the volume of trade are strictly controlled) and plan-guided goods (in which only the value of trade is controlled). In 1984, there was a reform of the trade management system, with foreign trade enterprises being given autonomy to deal with international trade. In 1985, the number of goods under these categories was cut to about 100 each. By 1991, almost all exports were deregulated, with only 15 percent controlled by specially appointed trading companies. Imports have also been deregulated. The proportion of plan-commanded imports in the total import volume was reduced from 40 percent in 1985 to 18.5 percent in 1991 (Wan et al. 2004).

Running parallel with the gradual acceleration of its economic reforms, China has also increasingly amplified its foreign-related legal system, steadily improved its trade and investment environment, and enforced the intellectual property rights protection system. With regard to the issue of trade system transparency, China has sorted out and publicized all management documents that used to be deemed confidential. In 1993, the Ministry of Foreign Trade and Economic Cooperation (MFTEC) was established to reform laws and regulations on the management of foreign trade and economic cooperation. Import restrictions were eased further. By 1994, almost all planning on imports and exports was abolished, with only a few exceptions where extremely important goods were traded by specially appointed trading companies. One year later, by the end of 1995, China had rescinded import licensing and quota controls on 826 tariff lines.

China's foreign exchange system used to be subject to rigid control by the government. Since the late 1970s, the foreign exchange system has been subject to a gradual process of liberalization. In the early 1980s, Chinese currency RMB was non-convertible and foreign exchanges were strictly supervised by the state. During this period two exchange rates were in operation: an official rate published by the government and another special one for foreign trade. The intention of the system was to enhance the country's exports and to restrict its imports, for at the time China was suffering from a serious lack of foreign exchange. In 1984, a new policy of retaining exchange was adopted by the government as a result of improvements in China's foreign trade and economy. It allowed domestic enterprises and institutions to retain a part of their foreign currency earnings, compared with the previous one in which these units handed over all of their foreign currency earnings to the state. Although a large part of foreign exchange was still under the control of the government, the new retaining policy stimulated domestic enterprises to increase their exports, and hence there was a significant improvement in China's foreign trade performance. On January 1, 1994, China established a new unitary and floating exchange-rate system. Although it is based on market supply and demand, this system is still, to a large extent, determined by the government, as the People's Bank of China (PBC), China's central bank, takes the position of the largest demander of foreign exchange and the Bank of China (BOC), which is also owned by the state, is the largest supplier of foreign exchange. Furthermore, the newly established foreign exchange rate system is still officially controlled and the central bank is one of the biggest participants in the market in order to maintain the RMB rate at a reasonable level.

In pre-reform China, tariffs were high and represented the only form of protection. When China initiated significant trade reforms in 1992, the rates of tariff were still high, averaging 44.05 percent. Since 1992, China has cut its tariff rates substantially every year. For example, the average tariff rate fell to 17.1 percent in 1998. On the other hand, non-tariff barriers were introduced in the early 1980s. Subsequently, an increasing number of goods were placed under licensed trading and quota. In 1992, some 25 percent of imports and 15 percent of exports were managed under licenses. However, the scope of license and quota management has been narrowed down since 1992. By 1997, only 384 categories of imports, only 5 percent of the total, were managed under quota and licenses. China's import-regulating tax system was finally abolished in 1992. Since this time, the Chinese government has reduced the tariffs on three occasions. However, the average tariff rate was still higher than that of other developing countries before April 1996 when

China began to reduce the tariff rates on more than 4,000 items of imported commodities with an average reduction of over 30 percent. Meanwhile, tax exemption and reduction for the foreign-funded enterprises have been abolished. After the reduction, China's average tariff rate was cut to 23 percent from the previous level.[2]

On December 11, 2001, China became the 143rd member of the WTO at the Fourth Ministerial Conference of the World Trade Organization (WTO) held in Doha, Qatar. In order to accede to the WTO, China agreed to take concrete steps to remove trade barriers and open up its markets to foreign companies and their exports in virtually every product sector and for a wide range of services as represented in the Protocol of Accession of the People's Republic of China (Document No. WT/L/432, 2001). With China's consent, the WTO created a special multilateral mechanism for the purpose of reviewing China's compliance on an annual basis. Known as the Transitional Review Mechanism, this mechanism operated annually for eight years after China's accession, with a final review by the tenth year. The WTO membership gave China an improved external environment under which the import of new technologies and capital inflows have given a boost to its industry. Exports have also been growing faster as China has been less strictly bound by trade quotas. For the first time in the last few decades China no longer needs to be concerned about the annual renewal of its most-favored nation (MFN) status by the US Congress. Furthermore, in accordance with WTO requirements, banks, insurance companies, telecommunications, and other service industries of the rest of the world will be allowed to operate in China according to the negotiated timetable. The impact may eventually break up the status of monopoly and state control that has existed in China for around half a century. In the long run the impact on social and political reforms can be highly significant.

On January 1, 2002, China cut the import tariffs on more than 5,000 goods. The average tariff rate was reduced to 12 percent from a level of 15.3 percent in 2001. The rate for manufacturing goods was reduced from 14.7 percent to 11.3 percent, while that for agricultural goods, excluding fisheries, fell from 18.8 percent to 15.8 percent (Wan et al. 2004). At the same time, China abolished the quota and license arrangement for grains, wool, cotton, chemical fertilizers, and so on. In addition, China modified or abolished those laws and regulations that are inconsistent with WTO rules. Since January 1, 2002, new laws on anti-dumping and anti-subsidy have been implemented. The average tariff rate was further cut from 12 percent in 2002 to 9.3 percent in 2005. Non-tariff barriers were also removed for most manufacturing goods by the end of 2004. Small and medium-sized enterprises and foreign-invested companies have also been entitled to participate directly in international trade.

A glance at the history of the PRC reveals that China's economic stagnation and prosperity have been closely related to its policy of economic internationalization. More specifically, when the autarkic policy was implemented, economic stagnation occurred; when the outward-looking policy was introduced, economic prosperity would be achieved accordingly. China's regional economic performances have also been decided in this way. Since the introduction of reform and open-door policies in 1978, China has basically formed a pattern featuring gradual advances from coastal to the inland areas (see Figure 7.1). This has also spread from processing industries to basic industries, infrastructure facilities and service trades, and is intended to develop toward a multi-level and universal opening pattern.

FOREIGN DIRECT INVESTMENT

The trends of FDI[3] can be distinguished according to changes in policy directions. During the late 1970s and the early 1980s, the Chinese government established four special economic zones (SEZs) in the Guangdong and Fujian provinces, and offered special incentive policies for these SEZs to attract FDI. China has made continuous efforts to attract foreign capital in the forms of both foreign loans and FDI. Foreign loans include foreign government loans, loans from international financial institutions, and buyers' credits and other private loans. In order to attract foreign investment, the NPC enacted the "Law of the People's Republic of China Concerning the Joint Ventures with

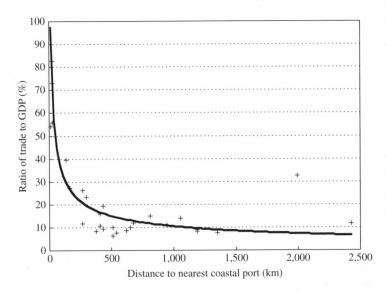

Notes
1 Data on "ratio of trade to GDP" are based on NBS (2002).
2 Data on "distance to nearest coastal port" are estimated by the author, based on the locations of China's 31 provincial capitals.

Figure 7.1   The spatial pattern of foreign trade in China

Chinese and Foreign Investment" in 1979. In the SEZs and other economic and technological development zones, foreign investors were afforded preferential treatment. Furthermore, the government assumes responsibility for improving the landscape and constructing infrastructure such as water-supply and drainage systems, electricity, roads, post and telecommunications, warehouses, and so on. While FDI inflows into China were highly concentrated in these SEZs, the amount was rather limited during this period.

Since the early 1980s, when 14 coastal cities across 10 provinces and Hainan island were opened, the previously recorded modest FDI levels started to take off. Total FDI inflows amounted to US$10.3 billion from 1984 to 1988, with an annual average growth of US$2.1 billion. This remarkable upward trend, however, dropped steeply in 1989, mainly due to the impact of the Tiananmen incident.

The growth of FDI inflows into China slowed down at a meager 6.2 percent level in 1989 and only 2.8 percent in 1990. Even though FDI resumed its growth path in 1991, by recording an increase of 25.2 percent over the previous year, the annual growth rate for this overall period fell to 11.0 percent, which paled in comparison with the 38.1 percent recorded from 1984 to 1988 (OECD 2000).

The third phase began in spring 1992, when Deng Xiaoping went on a tour of China's southern coastal areas and SEZs. His visit, whose principal intention was to push forward China's overall economic reform process and to emphasize China's commitment to the open-door policy and market-oriented economic reform, also proved to be a success in terms of increasing the confidence of foreign investors in China. China adopted a new approach, turning away from special regimes toward a more nationwide implementation of open policies for FDI. The government issued a series of new policies and regulations to encourage FDI inflows. The results were remarkable. Since 1992 the inflows of FDI into China have accelerated and reached the peak level in the early 2000s.

Since it made its first calls for foreign capital participation in its economy in 1979, China has received a large proportion of international direct investment flows. China has become the second largest FDI recipient in the world, after the US, and the largest host country among the developing countries. China's position as a host to FDI is in fact too far removed from any other developing country—and most developed countries—to be placed under any serious challenge. China has been the largest recipient of FDI among developing countries since 1993. Joining the WTO in 2001 provided a strong push for a new wave of foreign investment into China. In 2003, China overtook the US as the world's biggest recipient, attracting a figure of US$53 billion. By the end of 2004, the number of established foreign-invested enterprises had reached more than half a million, with contracted foreign investment of more than US$1,000 billion and an actual foreign investment of more than US$500 billion (NBS 2005). This is the equivalent of 10 percent of direct investment worldwide and about 30 percent of the combined investment amount for all developing countries.

The three major forms of foreign investment in China are: joint venture, cooperative, and foreign enterprises. The scope of foreign investment has now extended from investments in tourism, textile, and building industries to cooperative ventures in oil exploration, transportation, telecommunications, machine building, electronics, and other industries. In summary, the major effects of foreign direct investment (FDI) on the Chinese economy are:

- increased trade growth and participation in the international segmentation of production;
- better dynamic specialization;
- increased export competitiveness;
- an important source of capital;
- more jobs, upgraded skills, and higher wages for employees;
- higher factor productivity and increased technology transfer;
- improvement of China's industrial structure;
- increased domestic competition;
- higher industrial performance.

Regarding the origins of FDI in 1995, Hong Kong and Macau were the largest investors and contributed 43.30 percent of the total foreign investment, followed by Japan (10.62 percent), Taiwan (6.58 percent), the US (6.51 percent), Singapore (3.87 percent), South Korea (2.47 percent), and the UK (2.10 percent). In 2005, the top 10 countries and regions with investments in China were as follows (in order of shares): Hong Kong, Virgin Islands, South Korea, Japan, the US, Taiwan, Singapore, Cayman Islands, West Samoa, and Germany, the total of which accounted for more than 80 percent the total actual use of foreign investments in the country.[4]

During the 1980s, FDI was concentrated in traditional labor-intensive manufacturing industries (light industry), especially textiles, garments, and real estate companies. Since 1992 it has gradually shifted to capital- and technology-intensive sectors, such as chemicals, machinery, transport equipment, electronics, and telecommunications. In the second half of the 1990s, while there was stagnation in foreign investments in traditional labor-intensive manufacturing industries, the IT industry became a new focus of investment. Investments in technology-intensive industries have become a new focus of investment. The goal to attract FDI inflows has been to introduce advanced technology, improve management, and expand markets. The modes of foreign investment have undergone some systematic changes. The basic option in the early period of reform was to set up a contractual joint venture. Since 1986, equity joint ventures and wholly foreign-owned enterprise investments have become the main forms of foreign investment. Since the 1990s, the share of wholly foreign-invested enterprises has increased gradually, as has the level of foreign control of joint ventures. By 2000, the actual investment share of wholly foreign-owned enterprises exceeded that of joint ventures; the former became the main force in impelling growth in foreign trade. A related fact is that, with the exception of a few sectors, the Chinese government repealed restrictions on foreign control in joint ventures.

Foreign investment has been unevenly distributed in China. FDI inflows have been heavily concentrated in China's coastal provinces, while the Central and Western regions have attracted only marginal shares. By 2000, foreign investments were felt in all parts of China, except in Tibet. Throughout the period the southeast coastal area has dominated as a recipient of inward foreign investment. Not surprisingly, the most important determinant for the irregular absorption of foreign capital is geographical location. For example, the Eastern belt received most of the foreign capital, while less than 10 percent of the total foreign capital flowed into the Central and Western belts, which cover more than 85 percent of China's territory. Nevertheless, this uneven pattern has improved gradually as a result of the government efforts to internationalize the inland economy.

This inequality stems from the FDI policies taken by the Chinese authority. The open-door policy began with the creation of SEZs and preferential regimes for 14 coastal cities. This has resulted in an overwhelming concentration of FDI in the east. With the adoption of more broad-based economic reforms and open-door policies for FDI in the 1990s, FDI inflows into China have started to spread to other provinces. Among the eastern region provinces, Guangdong's performance in attracting FDI has been particularly impressive. Its share of accumulated FDI stock from 1983 to 1998 was 29.4 percent of the national total, far exceeding all other provinces including Jiangsu and Fujian, each of which possessed around 10 percent of the national total, and ranked second and third among China's thirty provinces. However, if we analyze this province group one step further, we find that the shares of each province have changed gradually. The share of Guangdong has declined from 46.13 percent in the 1980s to 27.98 percent in the 1990s. In contrast, the shares of other coastal provinces (such as Jiangsu, Fujian, Zhejiang, Shandong, Tianjin, and Hubei) have increased steadily.

In recent years the share of the central provinces in the national total of accumulated FDI stocks has increased gradually—from 5.3 percent during the 1980s to 9.2 percent during the 1990s. The main contributors are Henan, Hubei, and Hunan provinces, with their shares of accumulated FDI in the national total doubling between the 1980s and the 1990s. These figures suggest that the provincial distribution of FDI inflows has spread somewhat from the opened coastal provinces into the inland provinces. The western, less developed provinces received only a very small amount of FDI inflows, with their share in the national accumulated FDI stocks declining from 4.7 percent in the 1980s to 3.2 percent in the 1990s. However, Sichuan and Shaanxi attracted relatively higher levels of FDI inflows than the other provinces in this group. In the final analysis, FDI inflows in the 1990s have diffused from the initially concentrated southern coastal areas toward the southeastern and eastern coastal areas, as well as toward inland areas. The three provincial groups of the Eastern, Central, and Western belts experienced different patterns of FDI inflows. For the eastern region provinces FDI inflows have been increasing steadily. For the other two provincial groups, the inflows of FDI have been much lower, especially for the western region provinces. As a result, in terms of the absolute magnitude of annual FDI inflows the gap between the Eastern belt and the Central and Western belts has actually broadened.

Foreign investment has played an increasing role in the Chinese economy. What is more important, the foreign enterprises have promoted the importation of advanced technology, equipment, and management, and, above all, competition mechanisms from the advanced economies. The foreign-invested enterprises (FIEs) have generated a considerable portion of China's total tax revenues and millions of job opportunities in the urban areas.

During the 1980s and early 1990s, most of the foreign investments came from small and medium-sized enterprises based in Hong Kong. The dominant position of Hong Kong is apparent from several factors. First, Hong Kong is geographically adjacent to Guangdong province, where Shenzhen—the most important SEZ of China—is located. Second, it was in the 1980s that Hong Kong made the transfer of its export-oriented labor-intensive manufacturing industry to mainland China. This is the typical "Flying Geese Paradigm" of the international division of labor. Third, especially since 1992, investments from Hong Kong took advantage of the preferential treatment given to foreign investors.

FOREIGN TRADE

In *The Wealth of Nations*, Adam Smith (1776) explained not only the critical role that the market played in the relocation of a nation's resources, but also the nature of the social order that it achieved and helped to maintain. Applying his ideas about economic activity within a country to specialization and exchange between countries, Smith concluded that countries should specialize in and export those commodities in which they had an advantage and should import those commodities in which the trading partner had an advantage. Each country should export those commodities it produced more efficiently because the absolute labor required per unit was less than that of the prospective trading partner. According to Smith, there is a basis for trade because nations are clearly better off specializing in their lower cost commodities and importing those commodities that can be produced more cheaply abroad.

In the early days of the PRC, China's foreign trade reflected, to a large extent, the basic characteristics of a socialist economy. To bring about socialist modernization in its own way, China did not adopt the strategy of "founding a nation on trade" used by many industrially developed nations; rather, it was based on the principle of "independence and self-reliance" during the first decades of the PRC. As a result, China lagged far behind advanced nations. In order to achieve rapid economic modernization, the Chinese government has clearly recognized the importance of seeking new technologies through foreign trade and international cooperation.

China's foreign economic affairs had not been guided by a *laissez-faire* approach before, not even during the early stage of the reform era. Intervention in the form of trade restrictions such as tariffs and licensing, subsidies, tax incentives, and active contact with the world economy occurs in both imports and exports. China used to manage its foreign trade through a policy of high tariff rates. This policy had effectively promoted the development of China's immature, domestic industries. However, it also had a negative effect on the Chinese economy. For example, under the system of high tariff rates, products made abroad do not have the same opportunity to enter the Chinese market as those products made in China, which will inevitably prevent the importation of high-quality and cheap commodities from advanced nations, thus harming the interests of Chinese consumers, and finally providing fewer incentives for Chinese producers to improve their competitiveness.

In the 1950s, because of a trade embargo imposed by the US and other Western nations, most foreign trade was restricted to the countries of the Soviet bloc. Following the Sino–Soviet split in the early 1960s, there was a dramatic decrease in the level of foreign trade. Guided by the principle of "self-reliance and independence," China's foreign trade and economic relations were not improved significantly before the early

1970s. Since then, its trade with the capitalist market increased gradually, as a result of the *rapprochement* with Japan, the US, and some EU countries. However, because the autarkic economic policy was still in operation before the late 1970s, the volume of Chinese foreign trade and its ratio to GNP were still very small at that time.

Since the late 1970s, China has made many efforts to import advanced production equipment from abroad in order to use it to kick-start its economic takeoff. Except for a few years such as 1982–83 and 1989–90, China's foreign trade during the reform period has grown with exceptional rapidity. In 1978, China ranked 32nd in the world in terms of international trade. Its ranking improved to 15th in 1989, 10th in 1997, 6th in 2001, and, after exceeding that of Germany, 1st in 2009. The ratio of international trade to GDP also rose from less than 10 percent in 1978 to as high as more than 50 percent in 2004. As of 2007, China's top five trading partners, measured by the total trade volume, are the US, Japan, Hong Kong (including re-exports), Republic of Korea, and Taiwan (see Figure 7.2).

During the early period of the PRC, the Chinese economy sustained a large trade deficit. This seems to be reasonable because, after many years of wars, China's demand for both more consumer goods and also production materials was greater than it could possibly supply. From 1955 to 1977, China obtained a high level of trade surplus, with the exceptions of 1960, 1970, and 1974–75. Obviously, this beneficial foreign trade pattern had to a large extent been shaped by China's "self-reliance" policy for much of that period. China's attempt at speeding up economic development based on the "imported" method was mainly responsible for the trade deficit in the late 1970s. Trade deficit persisted between 1984 and 1989. Trade surplus has accompanied the strong and growing exports since 1990, with the exception of 1993 (see Figure 7.3). This has also increased China's foreign deposits. However, this trade surplus has also led to large trade deficits for its trade partners, sometimes resulting in retaliations.

China's increasing economic competitiveness and its growing goods exports have raised concerns in the Western nations. Over

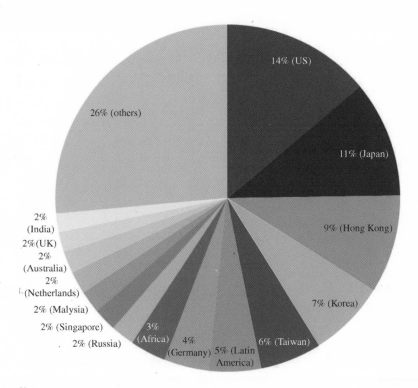

Notes
1 Data are as of 2008.
2 Hong Kong's share includes re-exports.

Figure 7.2   China's major trading partners

the past decade, a number of specific trade issues—textiles (the infamous "bra wars"), leather shoes, and car parts—have seen responses from the EU and the US that have been characterized as "protectionist." While divisions over policy responses have been seen between EU member states and different industries, trade policy is agreed at EU level and reflects compromise positions. EU Trade Commissioner Peter Mandelson identified China as "the biggest single challenge of globalization in the trade field [. . .] Europe must get China right—as a threat, an opportunity, and a prospective partner" (Mandelson 2009). Fears of China as a competitor have been most

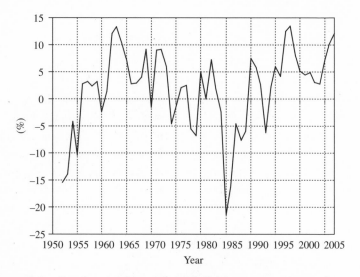

Figure 7.3   Foreign trade surplus (deficit) as percentage of total trade

obvious in the US. The US trade deficit on goods with China has grown in recent years. According to *Foreign Trade Statistics*, released by the US Census Bureau, in 2005 the total deficit was US$201.6 billion, compared with US$161.9 billion in 2004; US$83.8 billion in 2000; and US$18.3 billion in 1992. The US–China deficit on goods of US$201.6 billion was equivalent to 26.3 percent of the value of the total US trade in goods deficit in 2005.

Generally, foreign trade can be classified into four types according to the composition of imported and exported commodities in kind:

1. both imports and exports are dominated by primary goods;
2. imports are dominated by primary goods while exports are dominated by manufactured goods;
3. exports are dominated by primary goods while imports are dominated by manufactured goods;
4. both imports and exports are dominated by manufactured goods.

In recent decades China's foreign trade has effectively transformed from pattern (1) to pattern (4). In the early 1950s, the shares of primary and manufactured goods were about 80 percent and 20 percent of total exports, respectively. Since then, the share of manufactured products to total exports has grown steadily and it eventually overtook that of primary products in the early 1980s. China's export of manufactured goods has accounted for an increasing share since the mid-1980s, while the corresponding level of imports has declined, although at a slow rate. Clearly, China has been industrializing and is becoming a major exporter of manufactured goods. This structural change of exports has been largely ascribed to China's strong push toward industrialization since 1949. The composition of imported commodities includes a very small share of primary products compared with that of manu-factured products, as a result of China's abundance in natural resources as well as its large agricultural sector.

In summary, China's open-door policy and its quest for economic globalization have been the major driving force behind China's success. In this connection the roles of overseas Chinese, Hong Kong, and Taiwan are often emphasized. In addition, social and cultural influences of the open-door policy on the Chinese economy should never be neglected, since they also significantly determined the rates of economic development. Anyone who has ever traveled to western and inland cities cannot fail to notice that their vibrant local economies were due largely to their interactions with the outside world. More important is the great potential of comparative advantages as well as the close cultural linkages between Hong Kong, Macau, Taiwan, and mainland China.

ENDNOTES

1 Cited from *Guangxu Da Qing Huidian Shili* (vol. 775, p. 4 and vol. 776, p. 13).
2 Based on Yin (1998) and Wan et al. (2004).

3   In this section, only FDI inflows are discussed. China's FDI outflows, though small amounts at present, are growing larger at an annual rate of US$5.5 billion (Winters and Yusuf 2007, p. 23), mostly in Asia (especially Hong Kong), Latin America, and Africa. In fact, the net wealth of Chinese affiliates abroad can be measured in hundreds of billion dollars.

4   Calculated by the author, based on SSB (1996) and NBS (2006).

CHAPTER EIGHT

STUDYING CHINESE ECONOMICS: KEY ISSUES

The Temple of Heaven, central Beijing

China's modern development defies conventional explanation. In the late 1950s, the same authoritarian regime, which is now successfully leading the fastest growing economy in the world, was waging a massive campaign under the name of the "Great Leap Forward," which resulted in the loss of a large number of lives. From 1966 to

1976, the same regime was launching a so-called "Great Proletariat Cultural Revolution," causing serious cultural and economic damage to this nation. Furthermore, influential theories of the political economy of the former socialist systems emphasize that unless the one-party (Communist Party) monopoly is abolished, reforms are doomed to fail (Kornai 1992). Consequently, this will lead to a series of questions . . .

> *If you understand others you have intelligence;*
> (zhi ren zhe zhi)
> *If you understand yourself you are illuminated.*
> (zi zhi zhe ming)
> *If you overcome others you have strength;*
> (sheng ren zhe you li)
> *If you overcome yourself you are powerful.*
> (zi sheng zhe qiang)
>
> —*Daode Jing* (33: 1–4)

WHY CHINA HAS A COLLECTIVISTIC CULTURE

Individualism and collectivism are conflicting in terms of the nature of humans, society, and the relationship between them. Unlike the West, in which there exists an individualist culture, China has a collectivistic culture. Collectivism is the political theory that states that the will of the people is omnipotent, that an individual must obey; that society as a whole, not the individual, is the unit of moral value. Individualism, as the antipode of collectivism, holds that the individual is the primary unit of reality and the ultimate standard of value. This view does not deny that societies exist or that people benefit from living in them, but it sees society as a collection of individuals, not something over and above them.

Collectivism holds that a group—such as a nation, a community, and a race—is the primary unit of reality and the ultimate standard of value. This view stresses that the needs and goals of the individual must be subordinate to those of the group. Unlike collectivism, which requires self-sacrifice, individualism holds that every person is an end in himself and that no person should be sacrificed for the sake of another. While not denying that one person can build on the achievements of others, individualism points out that the individual is the unit of achievement. Individualism holds that achievement goes beyond what has already been done; it is something new that is created by the individual. Collectivism, on the other hand, holds that achievement is a product of society.

Then why is there a collectivistic culture in China? To answer this question, let us first analyze the key catalyst to the birth of Chinese civilization.

When considering the world's great ancient civilizations, we can find that most of them are centered in river valleys. The Sumerians were located along the Euphrates and the Tigris rivers and their tributaries, and the Egyptians around the Nile. Roots of the ancient Indus civilization originated along the Indus River, and the earliest Chinese dynasties centered their culture on the Yellow River. Not only were rivers used for irrigating crops and daily water needs, but societies also relied on the rivers for communication and transportation.

The hydrological characteristics of rivers heavily influenced ancient riparian civilizations. Large workforces were needed to divert water for irrigation and build protective works to minimize flood damage. This led to increasing sedentism, high population density, and the need for a centralized administration along the river valley. The development of "hydraulic societies" in China that were dependent on complex irrigation systems is a good example. The cost of hydraulic constructions and its subsequent maintenance required a political and social structure capable of forceful extraction of labor. Furthermore, upstream communities usually have a strategic advantage over downstream residents regarding the control of water. As a result, social stratification and armed military forces emerged alongside large-scale water control. These are very important processes in the development of ancient civilizations.

If ancient civilizations commonly originated along ancient river systems, then why did some river systems such as the Amazon, Yangtze, Mississippi, Volga, and Rhine not experience the rise of *in situ* socio-political complexity? This may be related to more local environmental and hydrological factors that influence the frequency and magnitude of natural disasters and create variable adaptive stress. Natural disasters have economic and emotional effects on people. The ability to predict and to combat or prevent natural disasters that threaten us is crucial in the development of human civilizations. However, not all natural disasters are the same, and they vary in how they can stimulate the development of social and political complexity. For the sake of brevity, I focus on the cyclic nature of riverine floods.[1]

One of the hallmark creations of early civilizations is the calendar. A device to mark cyclical time is not easily related to droughts, earthquakes, volcanic eruptions, famine, windstorms, and other natural disasters. Calendars were closely related to the regularity of river flooding. For example, in ancient Egypt the 15th day of June, or the start of the flooding season of the Nile, was selected as the first day of a new year. As natural disasters tied to flooding are more frequently found in large river valleys (especially in their lower reaches), people living in such areas developed technological tools in order to survive.

The growth of the ancient Chinese civilization along the valley of the Yellow River provides even stronger evidence which supports the hypothesis that civilization originates as a human response to river floods. China has had a particularly long and terrible history of devastating floods. More than 5,000 kilometers long, the Yellow River begins high above sea level in the Western mountain area and ends at the Yellow Sea. During China's long history, the Yellow River has been dubbed "China's Sorrow," because it has killed more people than any other river in the world. Much of the problem stems from the high silt content of the river. Millions of tons of yellow mud choke the channel, causing the river to overflow and change its course. Water is held in by dikes of ever-increasing height. In its lower reaches, the riverbed has actually become 20 meters higher than the level of the surrounding countryside. At the same time, the river has also been known as the "cradle of Chinese civilization" and considered a blessing with the nickname "China's Pride."

During the course of Chinese history, attempts to control the Yellow River have been categorized by different strategic approaches. One strategy is the active control of the river: to confine it within a narrow channel through the use of a system of high levees. More often than not, Chinese scholars have seen the close confinement of the river as a "Confucian" solution of discipline and order imposed upon nature—this contrasts with the "Taoist" solution of allowing the river a more "natural" course within lighter constraints. In either case, however, river engineering represented a tremendous interference with any "natural" regime; and the contrasting solutions were more accurately characterized as being opposites of engineering than philosophical approaches. Certainly, these contradicting phenomena are the defining results of the differing living conditions on which Confucian and Taoist founders were based (see Table 8.1). Specifically, the Confucians, including Confucius and Mencius and early followers, all of whom lived within the lower reaches of the Yellow River, had either suffered more seriously from river floods, or been more deeply impressed by such flood-related stories as told by their elders, than Laozi, the founder of Taoism. For example, the following story is included in the Analects of Mencius (372–289 BC):

> During the time of Emperor Yao [about the 22nd century BC], the waters, flowing out of their channels, inundated the Central Kingdom. Snakes and dragons occupied it, and the people had no place in which they could settle themselves. On low grounds they made nests for themselves on trees or raised platforms, and on high grounds they made caves. It is said in the Book of History, "The waters in their wild course warned me." Those "waters in their wild course" were the waters of the great inundation. Emperor Shun dispatched Yu

Table 8.1 Confucianism versus Taoism: Some Basic Facts

	Confucianism	Taoism
Founder's name	Kongzi (Confucius)	Laozi (Lao Tzu)
Founder's year of birth	551 BC	c. 600 BC
Founder's place of birth/living	Qufu—lower reaches of Yellow River	Luyi/Luoyi[a]—middle and upper reaches of Yellow River
How the founder suffered from river flood	Very serious	Not serious
Attitude toward flood control	Narrow channel by high levees	Wider flood plain between lower levees
Overall goal	Find peaceful and harmonious place of life	No overall goal
Rule of behavior	Follow a certain relationship between people	Follow the life according to the Tao

[a] Laozi spent most of his career first at Luoyi (capital of the Eastern Zhou dynasty) and later at the mountain areas in western China.

to reduce the waters to order. Yu dug open their obstructed channels, and conducted them to the sea. He drove away the snakes and dragons, and forced them into the grassy marshes. On this, the waters pursued their course through the country, even the waters of the Jiang, the Huai, the He and the Han, and the dangers and obstructions which they had occasioned were removed. The birds and beasts which had injured the people also disappeared, and after this men found the plains available for them.[2]

Subject to differing living conditions within the valley of the Yellow River, the Confucian and Taoist schools each has its unique view on basic beliefs, overall goals, the goals of individual behavior, the view of life, the rule of behavior, and views about society. The overall goal of Confucianism is to find a peaceful and harmonious place in life, whereas that of Taoism has no overall aim. The Taoists simply have to follow the life according to the Tao, but the Confucians adhere to certain behaviors and seek to be in harmony with nature. They believe that you should improve yourself through education and the development of your character, and that you need to understand the complicated relationships with your family members, with the government, and with society as a whole. Taoists believe that the life you live with the Tao is good and following the society's ways is bad.

Indeed, the Yellow River is the most important instrument to explain the differences between Chinese culture and the cultures of the world. The changes of the river's course have been spectacular, and the river mouth has sometimes changed catastrophically by hundreds of kilometers. It has had dozens of major and numerous minor changes in course in the past, each leading to great amount of not only human casualties but also property losses. These features have influenced the lifestyles of the Chinese people, especially those within close proximity. For example, on comparing the architecture of the Yellow River Valley and of the southeast provinces (such as Guangdong and Fujian), we find that the houses and other buildings of the valley, especially at the lower reaches of the Yellow River, are much simpler and, of course, less firm in structure, with fewer valuable materials. Since the majority of the Han population living in the southeast provinces are descended from those who immigrated from the Yellow River Valley, only geographical features can explain such differences. People living at the Yellow River Valley must have frequently abandoned their homes in order to escape from the unruly, disastrous floodwaters.

The Yellow River can provide us with more details about Chinese society. For example, the difficulties in securing sufficient food within the valley of the Yellow River, probably a result of the frequent natural disasters, have influenced the economical foundations of Chinese cuisine. In contrast to Westerners, the Chinese have a much smaller percentage of fat and meat as the main ingredient in their daily diet. This instantly reminds me of the hypothesis that it is the shortage of food in quantity and category that drove the Chinese to develop many cooking methods (including braising, boiling, braising with soy sauce, roasting, baking, grilling, scalding, deep-frying, steaming, drying, and salt-preserving) in order to *make* their food more delicious. In addition, the scarcity of food has resulted in a distinctive eating habit (that is, dishes are placed in the center of a table so that everybody can share the meal) in ancient China. In the meantime, the above conditions have also contributed to the development of a collectivist-style culture in China.

WHY CHINA ADOPTED A GRADUAL ECONOMIC REFORM

To understand the implications of the incentives for the implementation of a reform in China, we must make a point about the relationship between the radicals and the conservatives within the CCP regime.[3] Both Deng Xiaoping and his senior supporters in power had been victims of the Cultural Revolution (1966–76) during which Mao criticized them for economic liberalism. The special events of Cultural Revolution meant that—regardless of their liberal or conservative ideology—they must unite or, at the very least, must not challenge each other in mutually tolerable matters during the early period of reform. The evidence described below will demonstrate how Chinese economic reform has evolved from the collusion of the CCP radicals and conservatives (during the early stages of reform) to the collusion of all political, economic, and cultural elites (during the later stages of reform), as well as how this evolution has influenced the outcomes of the Chinese reform *per se*.

One of the initial challenges facing the Chinese leadership was to provide for the creation of a rational and efficient governing system in order to support economic development. In pursuit of that goal, the cult of personality surrounding Mao Zedong was unequivocally condemned and was replaced by a strong emphasis on collective leadership. An example of this new emphasis was the CCP's restoration in February 1980 of its Secretariat, which had been suspended since 1966. The new CCP constitution, adopted in 1982, abolished the post of CCPCC chairman—a powerful post held by Mao Zedong for more than four decades, thereby providing a degree of balance between the CCP radicals and conservatives.

The most striking feature of the Chinese reform during the 1980s was the collusive game between the radicals and the conservatives. In considering a reform strategy, the radicals must take into account not only the benefit from the reform, but also the political cost stemming from the possibility of losing their coalition with the conservatives. Since deterrence implies cost, the reform strategy that both players (radicals and conservatives) would find optimal to cooperate does not equate the marginal economic benefit with the marginal economic cost. Instead, a player's optimal strategy of reform equates the marginal economic cost with the marginal economic and political costs. In other words, it is political cost that creates a wedge between the efficient and optimal strategies of reform.

Although the strategy of pursuing faster reforms maximizes the radicals' gross payoff, it does not maximize its net payoff. The radicals would find it optimal to have a strategy involving slower reform in which the marginal economic gains from cooperation equal the marginal political and economic costs. For example, Li Peng's long-lasting political career as premier is one of the outcomes resulting from the collusion of the radicals and conservatives. In 1987, Li became a member of the Politburo's powerful Standing Committee, and a year later Deng Xiaoping picked Li to succeed Zhao Ziyang as premier after Zhao had become the CCPCC's general-secretary. This choice might have been seen as unusual because Li Peng did not appear to share Deng's advocacy of economic reform. However, it illustrated clearly that Deng had to seek compromises with the conservatives. Perhaps, this might be an early case of the *baiping* game.[4] In the following years we can still observe:

> After the death of Deng Xiaoping in 1997, Jiang Zemin must deftly play [his] various wings [both radical and conservative groups] against each other. In this scenario, Li Peng, chairman of the eighth National People's Congress (NPC), was selected to hold the No. 2 post of the Chinese Communist Party Central Committee (CCPCC), higher than that of Zhu Rongji—premier

of the State Council—during the 1998–2003 tenure. This was the first in the PRC's history that NPC chairman held a political rank higher than that of premiership. Moreover, a large number of non-Communist party and non-party personages were selected as state leaders with the titles of vice chairpersons of the NPC and of the Chinese People's Political Consultative Congress (CPPCC) in exchange of their support of the CCP as the permanent ruler of the state. For example, as for the 2003–08 and the 2008–13 tenures, China's state-level leaders have included nine standing members of the CCPCC Politburo (some of whom also held the posts of president, premier, the NPC and CPPCC chairmen) and dozens of vice chairpersons of the NPC and of the CPPCC. The total number has been the highest since the 1980s.[5]

As a matter of fact, during the massive mandatory retirement program that was facilitated by a one-time buyout strategy in the early 1980s, the outgoing CCP officials were partially compensated, in both economic and political terms. For example, a special name was coined for this kind of retirement, *lixiu*—literally "to leave the post and rest." After *lixiu*, retired officials continued to enjoy all of their former political privileges, such as reading government circulars of the same level of confidentiality. Some served as special counselors for their successors. As economic compensations, they could keep using their official cars with chauffeurs and security guards. In addition, officials under *lixiu* received an extra month of wages each year and extra housing that their children and grandchildren were entitled to enjoy after their death. Without that reform, in which many younger cadres were able to play an important role, the reforms that followed afterwards would have been impossible.

Past reform events show that in China the institutional improvement toward a market-oriented system followed a non-linear pattern. From the late 1970s to the early 1990s, China's reform indicated a recurring pattern of reform and retrenchment identified by a four-stage process: "decentralization immediately followed by disorder, disorder immediately followed by centralization, centralization followed by rigidity, and rigidity followed by decentralization," a cycle of "de-centralization (*fang*)–disorder–centralization (*shou*)–rigidity." As a matter of fact, the *shou-fang* circle represents the dynamic process of the political games between radicals and conservatives. Specifically, the *fang* (decentralization) was initiated by the radicals, while the *shou* (centralization) was insisted upon by the conservatives. As a result of their very nature (as stated at the beginning of this section), both radicals and conservatives have compromised with each other's ini-tiatives during most of the reform era.

In considering the profitability of more rapid reforms, the conserva-tives take into account not only the benefits that may result from the reforms but also the political cost stemming from the possibility of them losing their supreme position in society. Since deterrence implies cost, the reform strategy that both players (radicals and conservatives) would find it optimal to cooperate does not equate the marginal economic benefit with the marginal economic cost. Instead, a player's optimal strategy of reforms equates the marginal economic cost with the marginal economic and political costs. In other words, it is political cost that creates a wedge between the efficient and optimal strategies of reforms.

When dealing with the early reforms, it is necessary to mention other stakeholders as well as their attitudes toward reforms. Farmers and urban workers—two groups that benefited from the reform-driven economic growth—did not oppose the CCP, and the reform in particular. Intellectuals, especially those who had received Westernized training and been seriously mistreated during the Cultural Revolution, adopted a more critical stance. They had a strong desire for Western democracy. On the other hand, however, the CCP elites, especially the CCP conservatives, could not at all accept a totally Western-oriented reform (Kang 2002). Since the radical reformers had been much less powerful than the CCP conservatives at the period when most CCP seniors were still alive, their attempt at uniting with intellectual elites failed the during Tiananmen incident in June 1989.

It seems likely that, as a result of the disappearance of the CCP seniors and the conservatives on the one hand and the emergence of more young and Western-learning officials on the other, the Chinese reform should have become increasingly radical since the mid-1990s. What does the evidence tell us?

As the initiation and sustainability of a reform requires political, economic, and cultural support, the identification of interest groups and stakeholders of the reform in general, but especially those who are politically (and otherwise) active as allies and opponents of reform, is an important step toward the successful completion of the reform. An important distinction is whether interest groups and stakeholders are organized—in other words, whether they pursue their common interest jointly in a coordinated fashion. It is natural to believe that stakeholders will exert pressure on policymakers. This, however, need not always be the case, as not all stakeholders are organized. Because organized interest groups are better informed than the citizenry at large, they can provide key personalities (the government officials, and legislators) with intelligence of various kinds.

Beginning in the mid-1980s, the bureaucratic reform generated a large surplus of government officials. At the same time, many government agencies began to establish business entities, and bureaucrats became managers of these businesses. As a result, the phenomenon later came to be known as *xiahai* ("jumping into the ocean"). Since the early 1990s, *xiahai* has been an immensely popular phenomenon among Chinese government officials. By joining the business world, the former bureaucrats obtain much higher economic payoffs as well as a higher degree of personal freedom, despite being exposed to increased economic uncertainty. On the other hand, there is a high demand for those bureaucrats, since in the half-reformed economy many non-state enterprises need their knowledge and skills in order to deal with the remaining government regulations.

Since the 16th National Congress of the CCP, held in Beijing in November 2002, CCP membership has been formally opened to China's business elite. The removal of the clause in the CCP's constitution that officially prohibited private businessmen from becoming party members and serving in the government is intended to bring the CCP constitution into line with the reality of the party's character and social composition as it prepares to accelerate the pace of market reforms. In a rambling opening address to the Congress, Jiang Zemin articulated the class interests of the new Chinese elite. He called for the Beijing regime to persevere in opening up to the capitalist market and declared that the CCP should protect the "legitimate rights and interests" of businessmen and property owners (Jiang 2002). The formal opening of the CCP to different levels of businesspeople in 2002 represented a turning point. The fact that Jiang's "Three Represents" theory formalizes what has already emerged was highlighted by the year 2002 *Forbes* magazine list of China's 100 richest multimillionaires. One-quarter of those on the list declared that they were CCP members. In addition, many Chinese CEOs of private companies or transnational corporations also have connections with the CCP.

Since the mid-1990s, cultural elites (including noted intellectuals, popular entertainers, and ethnic minority-based social elites) have been establishing closer links with the political and economic elites in China. The factors resulting in the collusion of the political and cultural elites might include the following. First, the disappearance of senior CCPCC members has weakened the power of the conservatives since the early 1990s, while the younger political leaders are usually more highly educated than their predecessors. Second, after the Tiananmen incident, radical intellectuals were subjected to serious retaliation, most of them either fleeing the country or disappearing from academic circles. Third, the changing external environment (such as the collapse of the former Soviet Union followed by the unsuccessful "Big-bang" reforms introduced in Russia, and also the US transferring from standing against the CCP to against China) helped most, if not all, intellectuals to cooperate with the CCP and the government.

Several books have portrayed the post-Tiananmen period as one of intense political disagreement.[6] Certainly, this was true until the mid-1990s. Yet, disagreements since this time have been expressed increasingly through non-sanctioned means by non-sanctioned actors. The elite battles evident today are based upon illegitimate evasion, rather than legitimate contestation. Thus the politics of contestation—legitimate competition within the structures of the polity properly used by a range of agreed actors—remains absent. The earnestness of contestation in the early reform era has been replaced by a lack of ethical standards in compliance or the intrigue of crypto-politics in the post-reform era.

Among China's rural peasantry and the industrial working class, a seething hostility is building up over official corruption, poverty, the loss of services, unemployment, and the widening income gap between the rich and the poor. After several years of factional debate within the CCP, a consensus has emerged that the lesson to be drawn from the Tiananmen events is that the regime must build a solid base among the urban upper and middle classes, while making no democratic concessions to the masses. The government believed it could weather the opposition of workers and peasants by keeping them like "scattered sand"—that is, lacking any national organization or coherent political program. Commenting on the sentiment of the political establishment, Kang (2002) points out:

> There is a stable alliance between the political, economic, and intellectual elite of China. The main consequence is that the elite won't challenge the CCP and the government. The economic elite love money, not democracy. Their vanity will also be satisfied as the CCP has promised them party membership and government positions.

How has the Chinese reform been linked to the collusion of the political, economic, and cultural elites? First of all, faced by the example of the failure of the radical reforms in the former USSR, the political elite—no matter how radical they had been during the previous period of reform—has become increasingly pragmatic over time. In essence, they would now be more likely to choose a more

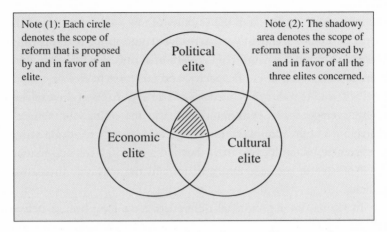

Note (1): Each circle denotes the scope of reform that is proposed by and in favor of an elite.

Note (2): The shadowy area denotes the scope of reform that is proposed by and in favor of all the three elites concerned.

Political elite

Economic elite

Cultural elite

Figure 8.1   Collective actions of the Chinese elites on reforms

gradual/partial (or alternatively, less radical) reform strategy than they had chosen in the 1980s. Second, the political, economic, and cultural elites have increasingly become beneficiaries of the existing system that was based upon the past gradual and partial reforms. As a result, there will be less and less incentive for them to see any (radical and thorough) political and economic reforms that could affect their existing benefits. Last but not least, in contrast to the reforms that had been merely decided by the political elite (including both CCP radicals and conservatives) before the mid-1990s, the reforms that have been decided by the political elite in cooperation with the economic and cultural elites since then have been far more limited in scope (as shown in Figure 8.1).

WHY THE CHINESE ECONOMY CANNOT BE SPATIALLY OPTIMIZED

According to the principle of spatial economics, the larger size of administrations can lead to risk-bearing economies. The underlying factor is that large administrations frequently engage in a range of diverse activities, so that a fall in the return from any one unit of the economy does not threaten the stability of the whole economy. While increases in size frequently confer advantages on an administration, there is a limit to the gains from growth in many cases. In other words, there is an optimal level of capacity, and increases in size beyond this level will lead to a loss of economies of size and manifest themselves in rising average costs. Without doubt, the increasing complexity of managing a large administration is the major source of administrative inefficiencies when its size grows beyond a certain level, and management of diverse socioeconomic affairs and risks become increasingly difficult.

In China, inter-provincial differences have long been a defining characteristic since in most cases their boundaries were created more than 2,000 years ago. In terms of its topography and physical environment, China is one of the most complex countries in the world. When glancing at a map of China, one will see that many provinces have natural geographical barriers such as mountains, rivers, lakes, and so on. This kind of geographical separation between adjacent provinces could have a serious effect on regional economic development if the inter-provincial transport and communication linkages are established inefficiently. On checking the highway networks shown in *China Atlas* published by the central and provincial authorities, we can observe that many highways do not reach the peripheral areas and, as a result, are not connected across provinces. Obviously, the fragmentary nature of the highway networks has exacerbated the inconveniences to the local inhabitant's lives and has had a particularly adverse effect on the Chinese economy.

Many provincial administrations have been informally demarcated in China. As a result, cross-border relations between the relevant provinces have never been easily coordinated and, sometimes, they can become a destabilizing source when it comes to social stability and economic development. Given the cross-border *imbroglios* between the provinces, the sustainable exploitation and utilization of natural resources (such as energy, metals, forests, fishery, and so on), as well as environmental protection in the border regions, will undoubtedly pose problems and disputes for both central and local governments. Non-cooperative cross-border relations between provinces could eventually become a source of disturbance to economic development. Even worse, some inter-provincial disputes led to armed conflicts and seriously affected the social security and economic sustainability in border regions. For example, most of China's inter-provincial borderlines are disputed and have even been published, according to their own preferences, by the provincial-level authorities in their official maps and documents.

One of the key initiatives of China's economic reform that began in the late 1970s was the promotion of decentralization in economic operations; that is, transferring economic management and decision making from central government to provincial and local governments. For example, retail trade, which used to be under the control of local government, is now determined by collectively and individually owned enterprises. Decentralization and the introduction of market forces together imply that the centers of economic power are moving away from central government to the localities. Since the advent of administrative decentralization, China's national economy had become effectively "cellularized" into a plethora of semi-autarkic regional enclaves. We will analyze this in detail below.

According to the principle of comparative advantage, the uneven distribution of natural resources and industrial structures among different provinces enhances the mutual complementarities of the Chinese economy. However, to a certain extent, administrative separation had formed a rigid self-reliant agricultural and industrial system for each province and had a serious effect on cross-border economic relations, particularly during the high tide of administrative decentralization stemming from economic reform. In some provinces, local authorities established, and provided finance for, a variety of schemes that promoted the sale of local products. Enterprises from other provinces, however, often have difficulties in finding office spaces, accommodation, or land for their business activities. These protectionist measures were, though in violation of central directives, occasionally enforced through a patchwork system of roadblocks, cargo seizures, ad hoc taxes, commercial surcharges and licensing fees, and in a number of well-publicized cases, highway robbery across the inter-provincial borders.

In addition, Chinese culture is not homogeneous across provinces, in terms of ethnic and linguistic groups (see Table 8.2). Geographically, the Han majority is dominant in the Eastern and Central belts with the only exception being Guangxi, which is a Zhuang autonomous region. The other minority-dominated autonomous regions include Ningxia (Hui minority-based) and Xinjiang (Ugyur minority-based) in the Northwest region, Inner Mongolia (Mongolian minority-based) in the North region, Tibet (Tibetan minority-based) in the Southwest region, and so on. More importantly, there are various religiously based areas in China. For example, people in Tibet and its adjacent autonomous areas in Southwest China usually adhere to Tibetan Buddhism, while most minorities in Northwest China have close connections to Islam. The Han Chinese, representing the majority of Chinese population in the Central and Eastern belts, are traditionally in favor of a mix of Buddhism, Confucianism, and Taoism, with the exception of a few of others. Naturally, it is unlikely that people with markedly differing attitudes, as well as different cultural values, could emphasize the adoption of a common standard and socioeconomic coordination.

In summary, in China the costs arising from the transactions between provinces cannot be underestimated. Among the factors that hinder attempts at coordination are the differing sub-administrative systems of Chinese provinces and their specific internal social and cultural conditions. Thus, the extent of progress in economic cooperation between the provinces must depend upon the extent to which the related sides pragmatically reorganize and respond to the economic and non-economic benefits and costs involved. Despite the mutually complementary conditions between many of its different regions, the Chinese economy cannot be spatially optimized since various geographical, institutional, and cultural barriers exist between most, if not all provincial administrations.

Table 8.2 China's Ethnic and Linguistic Differences, by Province

Province	Main Ethnic Groups	Main Languages
Anhui	Han, Hui, She	Mandarin
Beijing	Han, Hui, Man	Mandarin
Chongqing	Han, Yi	Mandarin
Fujian	Han, She, Hui	Min, Kejia
Gansu	Han, Hui, Tibetan	Mandarin, Mongolian
Guangdong	Han, Yao, Zhuang	Cantonese (Yue), Kejia, Miao-Yao
Guangxi	Zhuang, Han, Yao	Chinese dialects, Dai
Guizhou	Han, Miao, Buyi	Chinese dialects, Dai
Hainan	Han, Li, Miao	Chinese dialects, Kejia, Dai
Hebei	Han, Hui, Man	Mandarin
Heilongjiang	Han, Man, Korean	Mandarin
Henan	Han, Hui, Mongol	Mandarin
Hubei	Han, Tujia, Hui	Chinese dialects
Hunan	Han, Tujia, Miao	Xiang (Chinese dialects), Miao-Yao
Inner Mongolia	Mongol, Han	Mongolian, Mandarin
Jiangsu	Han, Hui, Man	Chinese dialects, Mandarin, Wu
Jiangxi	Han, Hui, Miao	Gan (Chinese dialects)
Jilin	Han, Korean, Man	Mandarin
Liaoning	Han, Man, Mongol	Mandarin
Ningxia	Hui, Han, Man	Mandarin
Qinghai	Han, Tibetan, Hui	Tibetan, Mongolian
Shaanxi	Han, Hui, Man	Mandarin
Shandong	Han, Hui, Man	Mandarin
Shanghai	Han	Wu
Shanxi	Han, Hui, Mongol	Mandarin
Sichuan	Han, Yi, Tibetan	Mandarin, Tibetan
Tianjin	Han, Hui, Korean	Mandarin
Tibet	Tibetan, Han, Menba	Tibetan
Xinjiang	Uighur, Han, Kazak	Turkish dialects, Mongolian
Yunnan	Han, Yi, Bai	Mandarin, Tibetan
Zhejiang	Han, She, Hui	Chinese dialects, Wu

WHY CHINA'S LONG-TERM GROWTH ISN'T SUSTAINABLE

Innovation has been the most fundamental element in promoting, either directly or indirectly, economic development and social change. In China, there were great thinkers such as Confucius, Mencius, Laozi, and Zhuangzi. But these achievements go back the periods of the Spring and Autumn (770–476 BC) and of the Warring States (475–221 BC), and there has not been a similar breakthrough within the past 1,000 years. Throughout its history, Chinese culture has two obvious historical traits. One is that it had a very long period of feudalism. The second trait is that the Imperial Examination (*keju*) system—which had largely promoted creativity and academic development during the Tang (AD 618–907) and Song (AD 960–1279) dynasties—was widely recognized as too rigid and deeply entrenched during the following centuries. In addition, the feudal period in Europe was shorter and was followed for over 200 years (from the fourteenth to the sixteenth century AD) by the Renaissance, a revolutionary movement in intellectual thought and inventiveness spurred on by the call to revive the arts of classical Greece. The Enlightenment and the Industrial Revolution that followed caused a tumultuous transformation in Europe. Shaking off its feudal shackles in ideology and social systems, Europe created a brave new world for itself. Under such circumstances, Europe produced many new creations and inventions in the realms of art, science, music, architecture, and so on. Over the course of the past 200 years, the US has attracted many high-caliber immigrants and provided very favorable conditions for creativity and inventiveness, making it the world's only present-day superpower.

Chinese culture, which aims to achieve a harmonious balance between Confucianism, Buddhism, and Taoism, had worked particularly well over a very long period. It is probably for this very reason that the Chinese remained intoxicated by past prosperity and still proudly regarded China as the *zhongguo* (center under heaven) of the world, even when it was beginning to lag far behind the Western nations. This kind of ethnocentrism and self-satisfaction eventually made China a typical autarkic society. The following were blamed for China's backwardness: the attachment to family becomes nepotism; the importance of interpersonal relationships rather than formal legality becomes cronyism; consensus becomes political corruption; conservatism and respect for authority become rigidity and an inability to innovate; much-vaunted educational achievements become rote-learning and a refusal to question those in authority; and so on. However, the same intellectual and social traditions, which were blamed for China's backwardness, have explained, according to some, the remarkable economic success in China and the greater Chinese region (including mainland China, Taiwan, Hong Kong, Macau, and other overseas Chinese communities in Southeast Asia). Are the Chinese prepared for dominance in what was to be the "Pacific century"?

In recent years, especially since Beijing successfully sponsored the 29th Olympic Games in 2008, during which China received the largest number of gold medals, the Chinese have been predicting when China will produce a Nobel laureate. This is a serious problem, which is worthwhile to inquire and meditate. Whenever the Nobel prizes are awarded every year, the Chinese will ask the same question since China's academic and intellectual achievements are not as noteworthy as its physical education. "Why do our schools always fail to nurture outstanding talents?" This is the question asked several times by Qian Xuesen—a famous scientist who received his university degrees in the US in the 1930s—before his death in 2009. Then, there was an open letter issued jointly by several professors to the Chinese Minister of Education and to the national educational circles. In contrast to China's recent economic achievements, there have been also serious concerns about China's political and economic sustainability. Then, how to explain the Qian Xuesen question?

Published in November 2009 by the Shanghai Jiao Tong University, the seventh annual Academic Ranking of World Universities (ARWU) offers a comparison of over 1,000 colleges worldwide. What is interesting is that the Chinese groups apparently made its study without bias. Unfortunately, none of the Chinese schools was in the list of the ARWU's top 200 schools in which Harvard University took the top ranking. The following phenomenon is more ridiculous. Since 2009, China has produced more PhDs than the US, making it the number one country holding doctorate degrees in the world. That is the good news. Less gladdening is that half of Chinese doctorates become government officials.[7] This phenomenon reflects a serious problem in China's policy on higher education. It is argued that this trend can only be harmful to social development. Producing so many doctorates to be officials—or, more specifically, awarding so many officials with doctorates—is in itself a misused function. Does one need a doctorate degree to be an official? From the perspective of educational development, this is an absurd and ridiculous phenomenon.

Since the late 1970s, a large number of university graduates and PhD students have traveled to Western nations to pursue their advanced studies. A majority of them, living primarily in the US, have remained abroad and these people constitute an important "brain-pool" for China's technological development. It is estimated that the total number of Chinese graduates now living in the US may be in the range of 200,000 to 300,000. Of these, around 10,000 to 15,000 are world-class scientists and engineers (Sigurdson et al. 2005, p. 65). Since the late 1990s, the Chinese government has sought to create a more favorable climate in order to encourage these overseas Chinese scholars to return home, in order to take over the running of laboratories, high-tech firms, or scientific parks. Yes, this kind of knowledge borrowing can recharge the batteries of economic growth for a short period. But, in order to achieve a sustainable, long-run economic development, China must be able to provide an academic environment in which the world-class talents will be produced endogenously.[8]

Although the Chinese government so far has managed the rising tensions between economic modernization on the one hand, and the many institutional flaws of authoritarian rule (for example, lack of political accountability, weak rule of law, bureaucratic ossification, and endemic corruption) on the other, China will not likely continue this course of rapid growth without undertaking the necessary political reforms to make the Chinese political system more responsive and respectful of individual rights. Indeed, it is no surprise that Chinese schools always fail to nurture outstanding talents. Now, China's colleges and universities have "no lack of money." They are able to build a campus that can give California Institute of Technology (where Professor Qian received his degree) "a sense of inferiority." But they are unable to produce an outstanding talent like Qian Xuesen. With so many universities competing to build luxury school buildings, there is still a lack of will to create an open and free academic atmosphere. So, when the executive power is always above the academic power in schools, and if the executive order is much higher than academic freedom, the Chinese schools will be unlikely to nurture outstanding talents.

ENDNOTES

1   In another book, I have provided an extensive analysis of the catalyst to the origin and evolution of Chinese and other major civilizations in the world (Guo 2009b).

2   Cited from Mencius (c. 300 BC, Teng Wen Gong II). Note that the term "dragon," which has also been known as the "God of water or rain" in traditional Chinese culture, probably was referred to as the beast "crocodile" or other amphibious lizards.

3   In fact, it is difficult to consistently identify the radicals and conservatives throughout the whole period of reform. Those who had been treated as radicals during one period might become conservatives at a later stage; furthermore, a CCP senior who can be a radical reformer with respect to one agenda (such as agricultural or other domestic sector reform) might be considered a conservative in another (such as external economic sectors or political reform in general).

4   Since the late 1990s, a new Chinese terminology—*baiping*—has been popularized in mainland China. The term *baiping* is composed of two Chinese characters—*bai* (to place, to put, to arrange, and so on.) and *ping* (flat, uniform, fair, and so on.). The original meaning of *baiping* is "to put flat; or to arrange uniformly." The term had been so informal before the twenty-first century that even the 1999 edition of *Cihai*—the largest and the most influential Chinese dictionary published by Shanghai Cishu Publishing House—didn't collect it. The frequently used *baiping* has extended from its original meaning to "to treat fairly." "to compromise," "to trade-off," "to punish," and so on.

5   Cited from Guo (2009a, p. 105).
6   See, for example, Fewsmith (1999) and Lam (1999).
7   Over the past decade, an increasing number of key Chinese officials—at both central and provincial levels—have been awarded with PhD degrees, regardless of whether or not they had academic qualifications.
8   In 1978, China's expenditure on public education accounted for 2.07 percent of its GNP. In later years, this ratio tended to rise gradually, reaching 2.69 percent in 1986, before dropping back to 2.08 percent in 1995 (Guo 1999). From 1995 to 2002, the ratio increased considerably to a level of near 3.5 percent; however, it has dropped again since that time (NBS 2008).

APPENDIXES

APPENDIX 1 A HISTORICAL CHRONOLOGY

1949   The People's Republic of China (PRC) is proclaimed. It is not recognized by the US and many other Western nations. The Kuomintang (KMT) still holds Taiwan and continues to claim legitimacy as the government of China as a whole.

1950   The Chinese People's Liberation Army (PLA) occupies Tibet. The Korean War begins.

1951   Chinese and North Korean armies occupy Seoul. The Tibetan government signs an agreement with the Chinese government in Beijing.

1952   The administrative divisions are readjusted in China.

1953   The first Five-Year Plan begins. The Chinese Buddhists' Association is established.

1954   The first direct Beijing–Moscow passenger train opens. China and India sign a joint declaration on principle of peaceful coexistence. The Central Military Committee of the CCPCC is established.

1955   China and Yugoslavia establish formal diplomatic relations. The new currency of RMB is issued.

1956   The tropical storm (named "Wanda") kills c. 5,000 people in Zhejiang province.

1957   The CCPCC puts forward the "Hundred Flowers" movement to allow limited freedom and criticism of the government.

1958   The "Great Leap Forward" movement. The People's Commune System (PCS) becomes a universal form of agricultural production. As peasants neglect their fields and try to produce steel in small-scale furnaces, agricultural production slumps dramatically in the following years.

1959 An uprising by Tibetans against Chinese rule is suppressed and the Dalai Lama flees to northern India with 10,000 supporters.

1960 The Russians withdraw their technical advisers and aid.

1961 The three-year famine ends, millions of people died from starvation.

1962 Border war with India.

1963 China's first computer (named "109") is successfully made. China's birth rate reaches a record high.

1964 Development of the atomic bomb.

1965 Tibet is formally made an autonomous region of China.

1966 The "Great Proletarian Cultural Revolution" begins. Universities are closed.

1967 China's Cultural Revolution movement reaches Hong Kong. China declares to shut down American spy planes.

1968 Liu Shaoqi, the Head of State, is imprisoned, dying a year later in jail.

1969 Border clashes with the USSR.

1970 Launch of an artificial satellite.

1971 The PRC is admitted to the United Nations in place of the Republic of China (ROC) regime in Taiwan. An attempted coup takes place, led by the Defense Minister, Lin Biao.

1972 US president Richard Nixon visits China. Japan establishes diplomatic relation with China.

1973 China and Japan jointly construct an undersea cable line in the East China Sea. China first convenes a national environmental protection conference. The 35th Guangzhou Exhibition, the largest exhibition ever in China, opens.

1974 China attacks the South Vietnamese army in, and occupies, the Paracel islands. The Daqing and Shengli Oilfields go into operation in North China, which is followed by the Dagang

Oilfield. The Chinese government calls for the implementation of population control policy.

1975 A new constitution is adopted. The position of Head of State is abolished.

1976 An earthquake of 7.8 on the Richter scale occurs at Tangshan city, Hebei province, on May 12, 2008, with over 200,000 victims. Death of Chinese premier Zhou Enlai. Mao Zedong dies and his widow, along with three radical members of the Politburo (the "Gang of Four") are arrested. Hua Guofeng succeeds Mao as party chairman and premier.

1977 Deng Xiaoping wrestles power from Hua Guofeng and is restored to his former posts. University entrance examination resumes.

1978 Third Plenum of the 11th CCPCC passes the "Decision of the CCPCC Concerning the Reform of Economic System".

1979 China sets up diplomatic relations with the US. The People's Congress of Guangdong province approves Shenzhen, next to Hong Kong, Zhuhai, next to Macau, and Santou as SEZs, to experiment a market-oriented economy. The NPC passes "Law of the People's Republic of China Concerning the Joint Ventures with Chinese and Foreign Investment." Shenzhen next to Hong Kong, Zhuhai next to Macau, and Santou are granted as special economic zones (SEZs). One year later, Xiamen, with close proximity to Taiwan, also becomes a SEZ with the approval of the NPC. The CCPCC and State Council grant Guangdong and Fujian provinces with "special policies and flexible measures" in foreign economic affairs.

1980 Hua Guofeng resigns as premier and is replaced by Zhao Ziyang, confirming the ascendancy of Deng's moderate supporters. Deng takes over as chairman of the Central Military Commission. The NPC grants Xiamen in Southeast Fujian province vis-à-vis Taiwan becoming a SEZ. China introduces the Household Responsibility System (HRS).

1981   The CCPCC chairman Fa Guofeng is replaced by Hu
        Yaobang. Deng Xiaoping puts forward the "One Country,
        Two Systems" policy.

1982   The post CCPCC Chairman is abolished.

1983   The CCP is purged of Maoists and those who oppose Deng's
        pragmatic policies.

1984   The CCPCC passes "Decision of the CCPCC Concerning the
        Reform of Economic Structure." The CCPCC and the State
        Council choose 14 coastal open cities. The State Council
        passes the "Provisional Regulations on the Enlargement of
        Autonomy of State-owned Industrial Enterprises." The
        State Council passes the "Provisional Regulations for the
        Management of 'Small-volume' Border Trade."

1985   The State Council approves Yangtze River, Pearl River, and
        South Fujian as coastal economic development zones.

1986   The Chinese government applies to resume GATT status.
        The NPC passes the "Bankruptcy Law Concerning the
        SOEs." The SOEs are encouraged to adopt the contract
        system. The State Council passes the "Regulations of Issues
        Concerning the Extensive Regional Economic Cooperation."

1987   Deng resigns from the CCPCC, but retains other influential
        posts.

1988   Hainan Island becomes a province and is approved as a SEZ
        with even more flexible policies. Liaodong and Shandong
        peninsulas and the Bohai Basin area are allowed to open up
        to the outside world.

1989   Former Party general secretary Hu Yaobang dies in April.
        Tiananmen Square becomes the focus and at one stage a
        million people assemble there. The PLA attacks the protest-
        ers. Zhao Ziyang is dismissed from his post as party general
        secretary and placed under house arrest. Jiang Zemin takes
        over as the CCPCC general secretary.

1990   Jiang Zemin succeeds Deng Xiaoping as chairman of the
        CCP Central Military Commission. Shanghai's Pudong area

is granted the status to enjoy some of the SEZ's mechanisms. The Asian Olympic Games are held in Beijing.

1991   Jiang Zemin calls for opposing "peaceful evolution." The NPC promotes Zhu Rongji to vice premier.

1992   Deng Xiaoping embarks on his famous Southern Tour and makes a speech on China's economic reform. China passes the "Measures Concerning the Supervision and Favorable Taxation for the People-to-People Trade in Sino–Myanmar Border." The Tibet autonomous region passes "Resolutions Concerning the Further Reform and Opening up to the Outside World"; "Provisional Regulations on Joint-Stock Companies"; "Notification Concerning the Further Opening up of the Five Frontier Cities and Towns of Nanning, Kunming, Pingxiang, Ruili, and Hekou"; "Some Favorable Policies and Economic Autonomy Authorized to the Frontier Cities of Heihe and Shuifenhe"; "Regulations on the Transformation of the Operating Mechanisms of State-owned Industrial Enterprises".

1993   Third Plenum of the 14th CCPCC passes the "Decision of the CCPCC on Several Issues Concerning the Establishment of a Socialist Market Economic Structure." The constitution is changed to confirm the State's aim of running a "socialist market economy." A modern enterprise system is introduced.

1994   The People's Bank of China separates banking from policy lending and reduces the number of the central bank's regional branches from 30 or more to only six. The introduction of a "tax-sharing system" into all provinces. The establishment of a new unitary and floating exchange-rate system.

1995   Policy of grasping the large and releasing the small is applied to Chinese SOEs.

1996   China tests surface-to-surface missiles in the sea off the coast of Taiwan.

1997   Deng Xiaoping dies in February. Jiang Zemin and Li
        Peng both announce that his economic policies will be
        maintained. Hong Kong is transferred to Chinese
        sovereignty.

1998   Amendment to Article 6 of the Chinese Constitution:
        "public, instead of state, ownership as the main form of
        ownership of the means of production." China signs (but
        does not ratify) the International Covenant on Civil and
        Political Rights. Dissidents attempt unsuccessfully to set up
        an opposition party, the China Democracy Party.

1999   Western Region Development Strategy (*xibu da kaifa*).
        Debt–equity swap scheme (*zhai zhuan gu*) in four large
        state-owned banks (China Construction Bank, Industrial
        and Commercial Bank of China, Agricultural Bank of China,
        and the Bank of China). The Falun Gong cult is banned as a
        threat to society. The Chinese embassy in Belgrade is
        bombed by NATO. Macau is transferred from Portuguese
        to Chinese sovereignty.

2000   Adoption of the "real name" banking system. The govern-
        ment publishes new rules allowing it to control material on
        the Internet. A census records the population at
        1,242,612,226.

2001   The International Olympic Committee awards the 29th
        Olympic Games to Beijing. The Shanghai Cooperation
        Organization (SCO) is established. A US spy plane is forced
        to land on Hainan island after colliding with a Chinese
        fighter aircraft. China joins the World Trade Organization
        (WTO).

2002   "Resurgence of the Old Industrial Base in the Northeast
        Region" is announced. The South–North Water Diversion pro-
        ject begins. China is by now the world's third largest Internet
        user, with a growth of 72 percent over the previous year.

2003   Transformation of the Bank of China and China Construc-
        tion Bank into joint stock ownership. China's first manned

aircraft is launched. The Three Gorges Dam project leads to the relocation of 1.5 million residents from the area. China records a trade surplus of US$44.6 billon despite the outbreak of Severe Acute Respiratory Syndrome (SARS). China overtakes the US as the world's biggest recipient of FDI.

2004   China decides to abolish agricultural tax within three years. Foreign investment in Chinese media companies is allowed under preconditions. China becomes the biggest trade partner of Japan, surpassing the US.

2005   The NPC passes the anti-secession law on Taiwan. KMT Chairman (Lien Chan) and CCP General Secretary (Hu Jintao) meet in Beijing. A new system is announced under which the RMB is pegged against a basket of currencies and will be allowed to fluctuate by 0.3 percent a day.

2006   "Freezing Point" (a weekly supplement to the *China Youth Daily*) is closed down and three editors removed from their positions. First oil from a new pipeline connecting China and Kazakhstan arrives in China.

2007   Amended property rights law passes at the 5th Session of the 10th NPC.

2008   An earthquake of 8.0 magnitude on the Richter scale occurs at Wenchuan county and its surrounding areas of Sichuan province, southwest China on May 12, 2008, with over 80,000 victims. The 29th Olympic Games are held in Beijing. Three direct links are set between Taiwan and mainland China. China becomes the second largest world exporter. Privatization of forestland for 70 years of tenure in selected areas. More flexible foreign exchange policies.

2009   China has now more than 360 million Internet users. Violence leading to death occurs in Muslim-dominated Xinjiang, with about 1,000 people (mostly the Han Chinese) being killed or wounded. China celebrates the 60th anniversary of the PRC at Tiananmen Square. China exceeds Japan as the second largest economy in terms of GDP, only behind the US. After exceeding Germany, China becomes the largest exporter. China becomes the largest producer and consumer of passenger cars and trucks.

APPENDIX 2 CHINA'S CULTURAL SIMILARITY WITH YOUR COUNTRY

Your Country	Religion (%)	Language (%)
Afghanistan	1.47	0.00
Albania	6.63	0.00
Algeria	1.47	0.00
American Samoa	5.95	0.00
Andorra	5.95	0.00
Angola	5.95	0.00
Antigua and Barbuda	5.95	0.00
Argentina	7.42	0.00
Armenia	0.00	0.00
Aruba	5.95	0.00
Australia	5.95	1.67
Austria	5.95	0.00
Azerbaijan	1.47	0.00
Bahamas, The	5.95	0.00
Bahrain	1.47	0.00
Bangladesh	1.47	0.00
Barbados	5.95	0.00
Belarus	5.95	0.00
Belgium	5.95	0.00
Belize	5.95	0.00
Benin	7.42	0.00
Bermuda	5.95	0.00
Bhutan	8.48	0.00
Bolivia	5.95	0.00
Bosnia and Herzegovina	7.42	0.00
Botswana	5.95	0.00
Brazil	5.95	0.00

Brunei	1.47	9.48
Bulgaria	1.47	0.00
Burkina Faso	7.42	0.00
Burundi	5.95	0.00
Cambodia	9.94	3.08
Cameroon	7.42	0.00
Canada	7.47	1.05
Cape Verde	5.95	0.00
Central African Republic	7.42	0.00
Chad	7.42	0.00
Chile	5.95	0.00
Colombia	5.95	0.00
Comoros	2.14	0.00
Congo, Dem. Rep. of the	7.34	0.00
Congo, Rep. of the	7.42	0.00
Costa Rica	5.95	0.20
Croatia	7.21	0.00
Cuba	1.47	0.00
Cyprus	4.96	0.00
Czech Republic	5.95	0.00
Denmark	5.95	0.00
Djibouti	4.20	0.00
Dominica	5.95	0.00
Dominican Republic	5.95	0.00
Ecuador	5.95	0.00
Egypt	2.47	0.00
El Salvador	5.95	0.00
Equatorial Guinea	5.95	0.00
Eritrea	1.47	0.00
Estonia	5.95	0.00
Ethiopia	7.42	0.00
Faroe Islands	5.95	0.00
Fiji	7.42	0.00
Finland	5.95	0.00
France	7.42	0.00

(*continued*)

Your Country	Religion (%)	Language (%)
French Guiana	5.95	0.00
French Polynesia	5.95	2.91
Gabon	5.95	0.00
Gambia, The	1.47	0.00
Gaza Strip	1.47	0.00
Georgia	1.47	0.00
Germany	7.42	0.00
Ghana	7.42	0.00
Gibraltar	5.95	0.00
Greece	1.33	0.00
Greenland	5.95	0.00
Grenada	5.95	0.00
Guadeloupe	5.95	0.00
Guam	5.95	1.45
Guatemala	5.95	0.00
Guernsey	0.00	0.00
Guinea	5.79	0.00
Guinea-Bissau	6.55	0.00
Guyana	7.42	0.00
Haiti	5.95	0.00
Honduras	5.95	0.00
Hong Kong	14.43	76.56
Hungary	5.95	0.00
Iceland	5.95	0.00
India	5.70	0.00
Indonesia	2.50	0.00
Iran	1.47	0.00
Iraq	4.48	0.00
Ireland	5.95	0.00
Isle of Man	5.95	0.00
Israel	1.47	0.00
Italy	7.17	0.00
Ivory Coast	7.42	0.00
Jamaica	5.95	0.00

Japan	9.17	0.34
Jersey	5.95	0.00
Jordan	5.01	0.00
Kazakhstan	3.58	0.90
Kenya	7.42	0.00
Kiribati	5.95	0.00
Korea, North	0.00	0.33
Korea, South	14.43	0.28
Kuwait	1.47	0.00
Kyrgyzstan	1.47	0.11
Laos	8.48	0.00
Latvia	5.95	0.00
Lebanon	7.42	0.00
Lesotho	5.95	0.00
Liberia	7.42	0.00
Libya	1.47	0.00
Liechtenstein	5.95	0.00
Lithuania	5.95	0.00
Luxembourg	5.95	0.00
Macau	8.48	92.06
Macedonia	1.47	0.00
Madagascar	7.42	0.00
Malawi	7.42	0.64
Malaysia	15.89	6.95
Maldives	1.47	0.00
Mali	2.47	0.00
Malta	5.95	0.00
Marshall Islands	5.95	0.00
Martinique	5.95	0.00
Mauritania	1.47	0.00
Mauritius	7.42	0.35
Mayotte	4.59	0.00
Mexico	5.95	0.00
Micronesia	5.95	0.00
Moldova	0.00	0.00

(*continued*)

Your Country	Religion (%)	Language (%)
Monaco	5.95	0.00
Mongolia	9.94	0.52
Morocco	1.47	0.00
Mozambique	7.42	0.64
Myanmar	14.86	0.00
Namibia	5.95	0.00
Nauru	5.95	4.35
Nepal	9.26	0.00
Netherlands, The	7.42	0.00
Netherlands Antilles	5.95	0.00
New Caledonia	5.95	0.00
New Zealand	5.95	0.00
Nicaragua	5.95	0.00
Niger	1.47	0.00
Nigeria	7.42	0.00
Northern Mariana	5.95	3.89
Norway	5.95	0.00
Oman	5.45	0.00
Pakistan	3.46	0.00
Palau	5.95	0.88
Panama	5.95	0.30
Papua New Guinea	5.95	0.00
Paraguay	5.95	0.00
Peru	5.95	0.00
Philippines, The	7.42	0.05
Poland	5.95	0.00
Portugal	5.95	0.00
Puerto Rico	5.95	0.00
Qatar	1.47	0.00
Reunion	7.42	1.98
Romania	5.01	0.00
Russia	2.38	0.10
Rwanda	6.98	0.00
St. Kitts and Nevis	5.95	0.00

St. Lucia	5.95	0.00
St. Vincent and the Grenadines	5.95	0.00
Samoa	5.95	0.00
San Marino	5.95	0.00
Sao Tome and Principe	5.95	0.00
Saudi Arabia	1.47	0.00
Senegal	3.49	0.00
Seychelles	5.95	0.00
Sierra Leone	7.42	0.00
Singapore	15.89	56.26
Slovakia	5.95	0.00
Slovenia	5.95	0.00
Solomon Islands	5.95	0.00
Somalia	1.47	0.00
South Africa	7.42	0.00
Spain	7.09	0.00
Sri Lanka	15.89	0.00
Sudan, The	7.42	0.00
Suriname	7.42	0.00
Swaziland	5.95	0.00
Sweden	5.95	0.00
Switzerland	5.95	0.00
Syria	6.99	0.00
Taiwan	12.13	92.06
Tajikistan	1.47	0.00
Tanzania	7.42	0.19
Thailand	10.49	12.13
Togo	7.42	0.00
Tonga	5.95	0.00
Trinidad and Tobago	7.42	0.00
Tunisia	1.47	0.00
Turkey	1.47	0.00
Turkmenistan	1.47	0.10
Tuvalu	5.95	0.00
Uganda	7.42	0.00

(*continued*)

Your Country	Religion (%)	Language (%)
Ukraine	5.95	0.00
United Arab Emirates	1.47	0.00
United Kingdom	7.38	0.00
United States	8.20	0.77
Uruguay	5.95	0.00
Uzbekistan	1.47	0.28
Vanuatu	5.95	0.00
Venezuela	5.95	0.00
Vietnam	14.43	2.33
Virgin Islands (U.S.)	5.95	0.00
West Bank	7.42	0.00
Western Sahara	1.47	0.00
Yemen	1.47	0.00
Yugoslavia	7.30	0.00
Zambia	5.95	0.00
Zimbabwe	5.95	0.00

Source: Calculated by the author.

BIBLIOGRAPHY

Asian Development Bank. Research on Poverty in Urban China. Unpublished report, Manila: Asian Development Bank, 2002.

Chen, M. and Cai, Z. *Groundwater Resources and the Related Environ-Hydrogeologic Problems in China* (in Chinese). Beijing: Seismological Press, 2000.

Chen, Y., Cai, Q., and Tang, H. Dust Storm as an Environmental Problem in North China. *Environmental Management*, 2003, vol. *33*, 413–17.

CISNR (ed.). *Handbook of Natural Resources in China* (in Chinese). Commission of Integrated Survey on Natural Resources (CISNR) of Chinese Academy of Sciences, Beijing: Science Press, 1990.

Coase, R. The Institutional Structure of Production. *American Economic Review*. vol. *82* (September), 1992, 713–19

Cui, M. (ed.), *China Energy Development Report—2007*. Beijing: Social Sciences Literature Press (in Chinese), 2007.

Deng, X. Excerpts from Talks Given in Wuchang, Shenzhen, Zhuhai and Shanghai. In: *Selected Works of Deng Xiaoping* (in Chinese), Beijing: The People's Press, 1992, pp. 385–418.

Du, P. *A Study of the Process of Population Aging in China* (in Chinese). Beijing: The People's University of China Press, 1994.

Economist Intelligence Agency (EIA). *International Energy Outlook 2006*. London: Economist Intelligence Agency, 2006.

Fewsmith, J. *China Since Tiananmen: The Politics of Transition*. Cambridge: Cambridge University Press, 1999.

Ge, Y. Probe into Countermeasures: A Path to Reducing the Unequal Distribution of Incomes (in Chinese). Development and Research Center of the State Council, Beijing, 2000.

Guangxu Da Qing Huidian Shili, vols. 775 and 776. Beijing: National Library of China, no date.

Guo, R. *How the Chinese Economy Works—A Multiregional Overview*. London and New York: Palgrave-Macmillan, 1999.

Guo, R. Linguistic and Religious Influences on Foreign Trade: Evidence from East Asia. *Asian Economic Journal*, 2007, vol. *21*(1), 101–21.

Guo, R. *How the Chinese Economy Works*. 3rd ed. London and New York: Palgrave-Macmillan, 2009a

Guo, R. *Intercultural Economic Analysis—Theory and Method*. New York: Springer, 2009b.

Gustafsson, B., Li, S. and Sicular, T. (eds). *Inequality and Public Policy in China*. Cambridge: Cambridge University Press, 2008.

Higgins, B. Economic Development and Regional Disparities: A Comparative Study of Four Federations. In R.L. Mathews (ed.), *Regional Disparities and Economic Development*. Canberra: The Australian National University Press, 1981, pp. 69–70.

Hill, H. and Weidemann, A. Regional Development in Indonesia: Patterns and Issues. In H. Hill (ed.), *Unity and Diversity: Regional Economic Development in Indonesia Since 1970*. Singapore: Oxford University Press, 1989, pp. 1–7.

Hu, A., Wang, S. and Kang, X. *Regional Disparities in China* (in Chinese). Shenyang: Liaoning People's Press, 1995.

Jiang, Z. *Report to the 16th National Congress of the Communist Party of China*. November 8, Beijing: Great Hall of the People, 2002.

Kang, X. An Analysis of Mainland China's Political Stability in the Coming3–5 Years. *Strategy and Management* (in Chinese), 2002, No. *3*, 1–15.

Kaufmann, D., Kraay, A. and Mastruzzi, M. Governance Matters VII: Aggregate and Individual Governance Indicators, 1996–2007. *World Bank Policy Research Working Paper* No. 4654, Washington, D.C.: World Bank, 2008.

Khan, A.R. and Riskin, C. *Inequality and Poverty in China in the Age of Globalization*. New York: Oxford University Press, 2001.

Kim, K.-H. and Mills, E.S. Urbanization and Regional Development in Korea. In: J.K. Kwon (ed.), *Korean Development*. New York: Green Press, 1990.

Kornai, J. *The Socialist System*. Princeton, NJ: Princeton University Press, 1992.

Lam, W.W. *The Era of Jiang Zemin*. Singapore: Prentice-Hall, 1999.

Li, S. China's Urban and Rural Income Surveys. *Journal of Financial Economics* (in Chinese), 2004, no. *3*.

Liao, J. Size of Industrial Enterprises Operation and Choice of Technology. In D. Xu et al. (eds), *China's Search for Economic Growth: The Chinese Economy Since 1949*. Beijing: The New World Press, 1982, pp. 130–44.

Maddison, A. *A Retrospect for the 200 Years of the World Economy, 1820-1992*, Paris: OECD Development Center, 1996.

Maddison, A. *The World Economy: A Millennial Perspective*. Paris: OECD Development Center, 2001.

Mandelson, P.Wolfsberg speech on EU trade policy goals in 2006 and beyond. 2006. Available at: europa.eu.int/comm/commission_barroso/mandelson/speeches_articles/temp_icentre.cfm?temp=sppm096_en, 4 May. Accessed November 20, 2009.

Mao, Z. The Bankrupt of the Idealist Conception of History. In *Selected Works of Mao Tse-tung*. vol. IV, Beijing: Foreign Languages Press, 1949, 1975, pp. 451–9.

Mencius (*c.* 300 BC) *Analects of Mencius* (an English-Chinese edition). Beijing: Foreign Languages Press, 1999.

Minami, R. *The Economic Development of China: A Comparison with the Japanese Experience*, English edition London: The Macmillan Press, 1994.

Nair, K.R.G. Inter-State Income Differentials in India, 1970–71 to 1979–80. In G.P. Mishra (ed.), *Regional Structure of Development and Growth in India*. New Delhi: Ashish Publishing House, 1985.

Naughton, B. *The Chinese Economy: Transitions and Growth*. Cambridge, MA: The MIT Press, 2007.

NBS *China Statistical Yearbook*, various issues. Beijing: China Statistics Publishing House, various years.

NEAA China Now No. 1 in CO2 Emissions, USA in Second Position. Netherlands Environmental Assessment Agency (NEAA), 2007. Available at www.mnp.nl. Accessed March 12, 2010.

North, D.The Contribution of the New Institutional Economics to an Understanding of the Transition Problem. *WIDER Annual Lectures*, March 1997.

OECD Main Developments and Impacts of Foreign Direct Investment on China's Economy. Directorate for Financial, Fiscal and Enterprise Affairs Working Papers on International Investment, No. 2000/4. Paris: OECD, December 2000.

Ottolenghi, D. and Steinherr, A. Yugoslavia: Was It A Winner's Curse? *Economies of Transition*, 1993, vol. *1*(2), 209–43.

Qian, Y. How Reform Worked in China. In D. Rodrik (ed.), *In Search of Prosperity: Analytic Narratives on Economic Growth*. Princeton, N.J.: Princeton University Press, 2007, pp. 297–333.

Qian, W. and Zhu, Y. Climate Change in China from 1880 to 1998 and its Impact on the Environmental Condition. *Climate Change*, 2001, vol. *50*, 419–44.

Riskin, C., Zhao, R. and Li Shi (eds). *China's Retreat from Equality: Income Distribution and Economic Transition*. New York: M.E. Sharpe, 2001.

Savoie, D.J. *Regional Economic Development: Canada's Search for Solution*. 2nd ed. Toronto: University of Toronto Press, 1992.

Si, T. Coal Efficiency Set to Get Boost. *China Daily*, November 3, 2008, p. 2.

Sigurdson, J.et al. *Technological Superpower China*. Cheltenham, UK: Edward Elgar, 2005.

Smith, A. *An Inquiry into the Nature and Causes of the Wealth of Nations*. London: J.M. Dent and Sons, 1776; 1977, Book IV.

Smith, D.M. *Geography, Inequality and Society*. Cambridge: Cambridge University Press, 1987.

SSB. *China Statistical Yearbook*, various issues. Beijing: China Statistics Publishing House, various years.

SSB. *A Compilation of Historical Statistical Materials of China's Provinces, Autonomous Regions and Municipalities (1949–89) (quanguo ge sheng, zhiziqu, zhixiashi lishi tongji zhiliao huibian 1949–89)*. Beijing: China Statistics Publishing House, 1990.

State Council A Retrospect on the Reforms of the Economic System and the Prospects on the Basic Thought of the Future Reforms (*jingji tizhi gaige de huigu yu jinhou gaige de jiben shilu*). In CCPCC Party School (ed.), *The Basic Plans for China's Economic Reform, 1979–87*. Beijing: the CCPCC Party School Press, 1988.

Streifel, S. Impact of China and India on Global Commodity Markets: Focus on Metals and Minerals and Petroleum. *Draft, Development Prospects Group*, Washington D.C.: World Bank, 2006.

Sun, J. *Territory, Resources, and Regional Development* (in Chinese). Beijing: People's Education Press, 1987.

UNDP. *Human Development Report 2005: International Cooperation at a Crossroad*. New York: Oxford University Press, 2005.

UNDP and CDRF. *China Human Development Report 2005*. Beijing: UNDP and China Development Research Foundation (CDRF), 2005.

UNESCO. *Statistical Yearbook*, Paris: UNESCO, various years.

UNPD. *World Population Prospects: The 2006 Revised Population Data Sheet*. New York: United Nations Population Division (UNPD), 2007.

Wan, G., Lu, M. and Zhao, C.Globalization and Regional Income Inequality Evidence from within China. Discussion Paper No. 2004/10, UNU World Institute for Development Economics Research (UNU-WIDER), Helsinki, Finland, November, 2004.

Watts, J.Satellite Data Reveals Beijing as Air Pollution Capital of World. *The Guardian*, October 31, 2005. Available at www.guardian.co.uk/news/2005/oct/31/china.pollution. Accessed on March 31, 2010.

Williamson, J. In Search of a Manual for Technopols. In: J. Williamson (ed.), *The Political Economy of Policy Reform*. Washington DC: Institute for International Economics, 1994.

Winters, L.A. and Yusuf, S. Introduction: Dancing with Giants. In: L. A. Winters and S. Yusuf (eds), *Dancing with Giants: China, India, and the Global Economy*. Washington, DC: World Bank Publications, 2007, pp. 1–34.

World Bank. *China: The Development of a Socialist Economy*. Washington DC: World Bank, 1983.

World Bank. *From Plan to Market: World Bank Development Report 1996*. New York: Oxford University Press, 1996.

World Bank. *Doing Business in China 2008*. Beijing: Social Sciences Literature Press, 2008.

World Resources Institute (WRI). *World Resources 1992–93*. Oxford: Oxford University Press, 1992.

World Resources Institute. *Water Resources and Freshwater Ecosystems*. Washington, DC: World Resources Institute, 2003. Available at: http://earthtrend.wri.org. Accessed on March 31, 2010.

Wu, J. Understanding and Interpreting Chinese Economic Reform. Mason, OH: Thomson South-Western, 2005.

Wu, J. Saving, Investment and Economic Growth. In: X. Wang and G. Fan (eds), *Sustainability of China's Economic Growth*. Beijing: Economic Science Press, 2000.

Yin, X. *The Procedure and Effects of China's Reform of International Trade* (in Chinese). Shanxi: Shanxi Economic Publishing House, 1998.

Zhao, R. *Increasing Income Inequality and Its Causes in China*. In: C. Riskin, R. Zhao, and Li Shi (eds), *China's Retreat from Equality: Income Distribution and Economic Transition*. New York: M.E. Sharpe, 2001, pp. 25–43.

INDEX